200 super s

hamlyn | all colour cookbook

200 super soups

Sara Lewis

For my lovely father, Michael, who would eat soup
every day if he could!

An Hachette UK Company
www.hachette.co.uk

First published in Great Britain in 2009 by Hamlyn,
a division of Octopus Publishing Group Ltd
Endeavour House, 189 Shaftesbury Avenue,
London WC2H 8JY
www.octopusbooks.co.uk

ISBN: 978-0-600-61935-2

A CIP catalogue record for this book is available
from the British Library.

Printed and bound in China

10 9 8 7 6 5

Both metric and imperial measurements have been given
in all recipes. Use one set of measurements only, not
a mixture of both.

Standard level spoon measurements are used in all recipes
1 tablespoon = one 15 ml spoon
1 teaspoon = one 5 ml spoon

Ovens should be preheated to the specified temperature
– if using a fan assisted oven, follow the manufacturer's
instructions for adjusting the time and the temperature.

Fresh herbs should be used unless otherwise stated.

Medium eggs should be used unless otherwise stated.

The Department of Health advises that eggs should not be
consumed raw. This book contains some dishes made with
raw and lightly cooked eggs. It is prudent for vulnerable
people such as pregnant and nursing mothers, invalids, the
elderly, babies and young children to avoid uncooked or
lightly cooked dishes made with eggs. Once prepared, these
dishes should be kept refrigerated and used promptly.

This book also includes dishes made with nuts and nut
derivatives. It is advisable for those with known allergic
reactions to nuts and nut derivatives and those who may be
potentially vulnerable to these allergies, such as pregnant and
nursing mothers, invalids, the elderly, babies and children to
avoid dishes made with nuts and nut oils. It is also prudent to
check the labels of pre-prepared ingredients for the possible
inclusion of nut derivatives.

contents

introduction

introduction

As we become ever more conscious of the benefits of eating freshly made healthy food, and the financial and environmental consequences of the huge amounts of food that we waste, there could not be a better time to return to making soups just as our mothers and grandmothers did. A homemade soup not only tastes great, but also makes a few ingredients seem like a whole lot more. They can be made at a fraction of the price of a carton of chilled soup from the supermarket and from a huge variety of ingredients. And they are surprisingly quick and easy to make. Once everything is in the saucepan they can be left to simmer while you get on with something else, requiring just 10 minutes or so at the end to finish off.

In the following pages you will find soups to appeal to all tastes, occasions and seasons, from speedy soups that can be put together quickly after a busy day at work, to slow-cooked, hearty winter warmers, perfect for a Saturday lunch. There are elegant soups with dainty garnishes to impress dinner guests and refreshing chilled soups for the hot days of summer. The range of recipes and ingredients is vast and sometimes surprising: there are traditional meat and vegetable broths; oriental hot and sour soups; creamy smooth vegetable soups; chunky fish chowders; classics such as French onion soup; and recipes gathered from world

cuisines, such as comforting chicken soup with lockshen, Indian-inspired mulligatawny and the vibrantly coloured Russian borshch.

Soups are the perfect comfort food: healthy, packed with vegetables and, depending on the soup you choose, usually low in fat. Tucking into a bowl of steaming hot soup on a cold, dull day is like turning on the central heating from the inside and guarantees to banish the winter blues.

types of soup

Broths These chunky, clear soups are really a complete meal in a bowl and can be thickened with rice, potatoes or pulses and mixed with lots of diced or shredded vegetables. They can be made even more substantial with the addition of tiny dumplings or pasta towards the end of cooking.

Chowders These chunky soups originated in America and contain lightly fried onions and diced potatoes simmered gently with smoked or white fish, or a mixture of flat fish and shellfish in fish stock, then finished with milk or milk and cream.

Purées Probably the most popular, these soups can be made with a huge variety of ingredients gently simmered with stock then blended in a liquidizer or food processor at the end of cooking for a smooth, silky texture.

Bisques These rich soups are always made with fish and puréed at the end of cooking,

then generally mixed with cream or a mix of milk and cream.

Veloutés These smooth soups are thickened with a mixture of egg yolks and cream to enrich the soup at the end of the cooking time. To prevent the eggs from curdling, a ladleful of hot soup is mixed with the eggs and cream before adding to the main pot of soup. It is crucial that these soups are then heated gently and not boiled, just as you would when making a sweet custard, stirring continuously, so that the eggs thicken the soup rather than scramble.

Potages A French term used to describe unstrained soups either poured over bread or topped with a bread croûte. They can also contain rice or pasta.

Consommés Ultra clear soups that are rather out of vogue now. They are made with a concentrated beef stock that is then filtered through a jelly bag with egg shells and egg white to remove any scum.

homemade stock

The best soups are those made with homemade stocks. Traditionally this was made from the bones of the Sunday roast and flavoured with a few vegetable trimmings and herbs, as a way of making use of every part of a joint and using those scraps of leftover meat to make a hearty and filling meal. In today's age of recycling, it still makes excellent sense to use that scrappy-looking chicken carcass as the base for a delicious lunch or supper. And don't chuck out those refrigerator and vegetable-basket oddments, either: that slightly wrinkled carrot; those last few slightly bendy celery sticks; the stalks from that bunch of parsley or coriander can all be put into the stock. Add the odd bay leaf from the garden or the green leek or spring onion tops that are rather strong tasting and a sprinkling of peppercorns for extra flavour. The more you add the better it will be.

The secret is to add all the ingredients and then to bring the stock just to the boil, reduce the heat to a very gentle simmer so that the water barely shudders, then cook with the lid half on, half off the pan for 2 hours, or longer if you have the time. Keep the heat very low, as if it is too high you will produce a thick, muddy-looking stock.

At the end of the cooking time, taste the stock. If it seems a little thin, remove the lid and simmer for another hour or two to reduce the liquid and concentrate the flavours. Strain and leave to cool. Skim any fat off the surface of meat stocks and refrigerate the stock until needed for up to 3 days.

Alternatively, you can freeze the stock in a plastic box or loaf tin lined with a large plastic bag for use later. Seal, label and freeze for up to 3 months. Defrost at room temperature, or in the microwave if preferred, minus the bag tie if used.

chicken stock

Preparation time **10 minutes**
Cooking time **2–2½ hours**
Makes about **1 litre (1¾ pints)**

1 leftover **cooked chicken carcass**
1 **onion**, quartered
2 **carrots**, thickly sliced
2 **celery sticks**, thickly sliced
1 **bay leaf** or small bunch of **mixed herbs**
¼ teaspoon **salt**
½ teaspoon roughly crushed **black peppercorns**
2.5 litres (4 pints) **cold water**

Put the chicken carcass and vegetables into a large saucepan. Add the herbs, salt and peppercorns.
Pour over the water and bring slowly just to the boil. Skim off any scum with a slotted spoon. Reduce the heat to a gentle simmer, then half cover with a lid and cook for 2–2½ hours until reduced by about half.
Strain the stock through a large sieve into a jug. Remove any chicken pieces still on the carcass, pick out the meat pieces from the sieve and reserve for the soup, but discard the vegetables. Chill the stock for several hours or overnight.

Skim off the thin layer of fat on the top of the chilled and now jellied stock with a dessertspoon. Chill and store in the refrigerator for up to 3 days.

A duck, pheasant, or guinea fowl carcass or a ham knuckle can also be made into stock in just the same way. If you have a turkey carcass then double up the vegetable and water quantities specified above.

If you have a chicken carcass but don't have time to make it into stock straightaway, you can freeze it for up to 3 months closely wrapped in clingfilm, then packed into a plastic bag. Defrost it at room temperature then make into stock as above.

beef stock

Preparation time **10 minutes**
Cooking time **4 hours 20 minutes–**
 5 hours 20 minutes
Makes about **1 litre (1¾ pints)**

2 kg (4 lb) **beef bones**, such as ribs or shin
2 **smoked streaky bacon rashers**, diced
2 **onions**, quartered but with the inner brown
 layer still on
2 **carrots**, thickly sliced
2 **celery sticks**, thickly sliced
1 **turnip**, diced (optional)
2 **bay leaves**, **rosemary sprigs** or **sage stems**
¼ teaspoon **salt**
½ teaspoon roughly crushed **black**
 peppercorns
3.6 litres (6 pints) **cold water**

Put the bones and bacon into a large saucepan and heat gently for 10 minutes until the marrow begins to run from the centre of the bones. Turn the bones occasionally.

Add the vegetables and fry for 10 more minutes, stirring the vegetables and turning the bones until browned.

Add the herbs, salt and peppercorns then pour in the water and bring slowly to the boil. Skim off any scum with a slotted spoon, then reduce the heat, half cover with a lid and simmer gently for 4–5 hours until the liquid has reduced by half.

Strain through a large sieve into a jug. Cool then chill in the refrigerator overnight. Skim off any fat and store in the refrigerator for up to 3 days.

If you're not in the habit of roasting large beef joints on the bone, you can obtain the beef bones from your local butcher; he may even give them to you for free. Use the bones raw when preparing your stock. Lamb stock can be made in the same way from cooked or uncooked lamb bones.

fish stock

Preparation time **10 minutes**
Cooking time **45 minutes**
Makes about **1 litre (1¾ pints)**

1 kg (2 lb) **fish trimmings**, such as heads,
   backbones, tails, skins and prawn shells
1 **onion**, quartered
2 **leek tops**, sliced
2 **carrots**, thickly sliced
2 **celery sticks**, thickly sliced
thyme sprigs
1 **bay leaf**
few **parsley stalks**
½ teaspoon roughly crushed
   white peppercorns
¼ teaspoon **salt**
1.5 litres (2½ pints) **cold water**
300 ml (½ pint) **dry white wine** or **extra water**

Put the fish trimmings in a large sieve, rinse
with cold water, drain and then put them into
a large saucepan with all the remaining
ingredients.
Bring slowly to the boil. Skim off any scum
with a slotted spoon. Cover and simmer for
30 minutes.
Strain the stock through a fine sieve, return
it to the saucepan and then simmer it,
uncovered, for about 15 minutes until
reduced by half. Cool then chill in the
refrigerator for up to 3 days.

If you are adding fish heads, don't cook them
for longer than 30 minutes before straining, or
they will begin to add a bitter taste.

vegetable stock

Preparation time **10 minutes**
Cooking time **1 hour 5 minutes**
Makes about **1 litre (1¾ pints)**

1 tablespoon **olive oil**
2 **onions**, roughly chopped
2 **leek tops**, roughly chopped
4 **carrots**, roughly chopped
2 **celery sticks**, thickly sliced
100 g (3½ oz) **cup mushrooms**, sliced
4 **tomatoes**, roughly chopped
small bunch of **mixed herbs**
½ teaspoon roughly crushed **black**
   peppercorns
¼ teaspoon **salt**
1.8 litres (3 pints) **cold water**

Heat the oil in a large saucepan, add the
vegetables and fry for 5 minutes until
softened and just beginning to turn golden
around the edges.
Add the tomatoes, herbs, peppercorns and
salt. Pour in the water, slowly bring to the boil,
then half cover and simmer gently for 1 hour.
Pour through a sieve into a jug. Cool then
chill for up to 3 days.

If you have some opened white wine or dry
cider then you can add 150 ml (¼ pint) wine
in place of the same amount of water.

Mix and match vegetables depending on
what you have. Chopped fennel or peeled and
diced celeriac give a flavourful addition. Half a
red or orange pepper and a few dried
mushrooms are also ideal.

stock cubes & ready-made stock

In our grandmothers' day, it would have been unheard of to make soup with a stock cube; nowadays, juggling work with family life means that time-saving short-cuts are a must. Very few people make enough stock for all their cooking needs and while it is great to have a few handy-sized bags of stock in the freezer, most of us cheat and use shop-bought products.

While there is nothing wrong with using stock cubes there are some soups for which homemade stock is crucial, such as the light, delicate-tasting Chilled Lettuce Soup (see page 74), Vichysoisse-style soups (see page 64) or clear consommé style broths such as Italian Tortellini in Brodo (see page 208) or Chicken Soup with Lockshen (see page 214).

The strength of flavour varies hugely in shop-bought stock cubes, so choose cubes or powder that are low in salt and make them up with a little extra water so that their flavour is not overpowering.

More and more supermarkets now sell tubs of chilled ready-made stocks and for a special-occasion soup such as Crab Bisque (see page 132) or French Onion Soup (see page 226) they give a much more authentic taste. They are more expensive, but much closer to the taste of homemade stock.

get ahead

Soups make such a warming, satisfying lunch that it is well worthwhile to freeze portions away in individual plastic boxes or plastic bags for occasions when you don't have time to cook from scratch. So, rather than always having a sandwich at work, why not take a frozen pack of soup with you so that it defrosts while you work, then give it a quick blast in the microwave at lunchtime.

If you don't have many plastic boxes, line a rectangular loaf tin with a freezer bag, fill with soup then seal, squeezing out as much air as possible. Freeze until solid then remove the bag from the tin, rinsing with cold water to loosen the bag from the tin if needed. The frozen block then makes for an easy stacking shape in your freezer. Just remember to label and date it, so that you will know what it is when you come to defrost it. There is nothing more frustrating than defrosting an item expecting it to be savoury, only to find it is fruit purée or something else sweet instead.

reheating

Only ever reheat foods once. If your family is planning to tuck into a batch of soup at different times, then ladle the amount required at any one time into a smaller saucepan or microwaveable bowl and then reheat thoroughly, leaving the remaining soup in the refrigerator until needed. Don't add extra liquid until the soup is heated through, as many will thin again once hot. Keep a watchful eye on the heat if eggs and cream were used in the recipe; the soup needs to be thoroughly reheated but not boiled rapidly, or the eggs will curdle. Stir frequently so that the soup heats up evenly.

finishing touches

A swirl of cream – this always looks special, yet what could be simpler than to drizzle a tablespoon or two of double cream or natural yogurt over a bowlful of puréed soup? Alternatively you can drop small spoonfuls of cream into the soup and then run a cocktail stick through them for a teardrop effect, or add a spoonful of thick Greek yogurt or crème fraîche into the centre of the soup and then sprinkle it with a few snipped herbs.

Herb garnishes – a few finely chopped fresh herbs can be all that is needed to liven up a pale puréed soup, such as fennel vichyssoise. For a crispy herb topping, shallow fry a handful of sage, basil or parsley leaves for a few seconds. For a topping with punch try a sprinkling of gremolata – a mix of chopped parsley, lemon rind and chopped garlic – or salsa verde – a mix of chopped herbs,

anchovies, garlic and olive oil. You could make up some herb-infused oil, store in a bottle and drizzle over the soup at the last minute. Or you can cheat and add a small spoonful of ready-made pesto.

Citrus curls – tiny lemon, lime or orange curls can be sprinkled over the top of the soup for a delicate zing. Use a zester, or the finest section on a grater.

Spicy sprinkles – try a little freshly grated nutmeg, a few roughly crushed peppercorns, a few crushed, dried chillies for extra heat or a little paprika or turmeric for added colour.

Flavoured butters and oil – mix a little butter with chopped blue cheese, anchovies and chilli, garlic, lemon rind or freshly chopped herbs. Shape into a log, chill, slice and then add a slice to the hot soup just before serving. Alternatively make up some mayonnaise-based sauces and flavour with garlic to make aïoli, chilli for rouille, or lemon rind and juice for a citrus burst.

Ice cubes – for chilled soups, add a few whole or roughly crushed ice cubes for added texture and impact.

Croûtons – fry diced or sliced bread (half– one slice per serving of soup) in a mixture of butter and sunflower oil or just olive oil until golden. Drain on kitchen paper and then float on bowls of soup just before serving. Croûtons can also be flavoured with garlic or spices. For French bread or ciabatta, rub the fried bread with a cut clove of garlic or spread with a little olive tapenade, pesto or crumbled blue cheese. For a lower-fat option, bake croûtons sprayed with a little olive oil in the oven until crisp.

speedy soups

tomato & balsamic vinegar soup

Serves **6**
Preparation time **25 minutes**
Cooking time **20 minutes**

750 g (1½ lb) large **tomatoes on the vine**
2 tablespoons **olive oil**
1 **onion**, roughly chopped
1 **baking potato**, about 200 g (7 oz), diced
2 **garlic cloves**, finely chopped (optional)
750 ml (1¼ pints) **vegetable** or **chicken stock** (see pages 13 and 10)
1 tablespoon **tomato purée**
1 tablespoon **soft brown sugar**
4 teaspoons **balsamic vinegar**
small bunch of **basil**
salt and **pepper**

Cut the tomatoes in half, place them cut-side down in a foil-lined grill pan and drizzle with some oil. Grill for 4–5 minutes until the skins have split and blackened. Meanwhile, fry the onion, potato and garlic in the remaining oil for 5 minutes, stirring occasionally until softened and turning golden around the edges.

Peel and roughly chop the tomatoes and add to the onion and potato with the pan juices, then stir in the stock, tomato purée, sugar and vinegar. Add half the basil, season and bring to the boil. Cover and simmer for 15 minutes.

Purée half the soup in batches in a blender or food processor until smooth. Return to the saucepan with the rest of the soup and reheat. Season to taste, then ladle into bowls, garnish with the remaining basil leaves and serve with Parmesan twists.

For Parmesan twists, to serve as an accompaniment, unroll one sheet of ready-rolled puff pastry from a 425 g (14 oz) defrosted pack of 2 sheets. Brush with a little beaten egg yolk then spread with 3 teaspoons tomato (or basil) pesto, a little pepper and 4 tablespoons of freshly grated Parmesan. Cover with the second unrolled pastry sheet. Brush the top with a little more egg yolk, then cut into strips about 1 cm (½ inch) wide. Twist each strip like a corkscrew, transfer to an oiled baking sheet and press the ends firmly on to the baking sheet to prevent them unravelling. Cook in a preheated oven, 200°C (400°F), Gas Mark 6, for about 10 minutes until golden brown. Serve warm.

black bean with soba noodles

Serves **4**
Preparation time **10 minutes**
Cooking time **15 minutes**

200 g (7 oz) **dried soba
Japanese noodles**
2 tablespoons **groundnut** or
vegetable oil
bunch of **spring onions**,
sliced
2 **garlic cloves**, roughly
chopped
1 **red chilli**, deseeded and
sliced
4 cm (1½ inch) piece of **fresh
root ginger**, peeled and
grated
125 ml (4 fl oz) **black bean
sauce** or **black bean stir-fry
sauce**
750 ml (1¼ pints) **vegetable
stock** (see page 13)
200 g (7 oz) **pak choi** or
spring greens, shredded
2 teaspoons **soy sauce**
1 teaspoon **caster sugar**
50 g (2 oz) **raw, unsalted
shelled peanuts**

Cook the noodles in a saucepan of boiling water for
about 5 minutes, or until just tender.

Meanwhile, heat the oil in a saucepan. Add the spring
onions and garlic and sauté gently for 1 minute.

Add the red chilli, fresh ginger, black bean sauce and
vegetable stock and bring to the boil. Stir in the pak
choi or spring greens, soy sauce, caster sugar and
peanuts; reduce the heat and simmer gently, uncovered,
for 4 minutes.

Drain the noodles and pile into serving bowls. Ladle
the soup over the noodles and serve immediately.

For beef & black bean soup, reduce the amount
of noodles to 125 g (4 oz) and cook as above.
Meanwhile, fry the spring onion then add the red chilli,
ginger, black bean sauce and stock. Bring to the boil
then add the green vegetables, soy sauce and sugar.
Cook for 2 minutes as above. Quickly trim the fat off a
250 g (8 oz) sirloin steak, cut into thin slices and add
to the soup. Cook for 2 more minutes then ladle into
noodle filled bowls.

broad bean & chorizo soup

Serves **6**
Preparation time **20 minutes**
Cooking time **20 minutes**

2 tablespoons **olive oil**
1 large **onion**, roughly
  chopped
500 g (1 lb) **potatoes**, diced
150 g (5 oz) **chorizo**, diced
4 **tomatoes**, diced
300 g (10 oz) **frozen broad
  beans**
1.5 litres (2½ pints) **chicken
  stock** (see page 10)
salt and **pepper**
basil leaves, to garnish

Olive tapenade toasts
12 slices **French bread**
2 **garlic cloves**, halved
4 tablespoons **green** or **black
  olive tapenade**

Heat the oil in a large saucepan, add the onion,
potatoes and chorizo and fry for 5 minutes, stirring
regularly until just beginning to soften.

Stir in the tomatoes, broad beans and stock, season
and bring to the boil. Cover and simmer for 15 minutes
until the vegetables are tender.

Mash some of the potatoes roughly with a fork
to thicken the soup slightly. Taste and adjust the
seasoning if needed.

Toast the bread on both sides then rub one side with
the halves of garlic and spread with the tapenade.
Ladle the soup into bowls and top with the tapenade
toasts and sprinkle with basil leaves to garnish.

For homemade green olive tapenade, to serve on
the toast, stone 250 g (8 oz) green olives then finely
chop them in a food processor with a small bunch of
fresh basil, 2 garlic cloves, 2 teaspoons drained
capers, 4 tablespoons olive oil and 1 tablespoon
white wine vinegar. This tapenade can also be served
with crudités or tossed with pasta. Any remaining
tapenade can be stored for up to two weeks in the
refrigerator in a small jar with the surface covered with
a little extra olive oil.

celeriac & apple soup

Serves **6**

Preparation time **10–15 minutes**

Cooking time **20–25 minutes**

25 g (1 oz) **butter** or **margarine**

1 **celeriac**, about 500 g (1 lb), peeled and coarsely grated

3 **dessert apples**, peeled, cored and chopped

1.2 litres (2 pints) **chicken or vegetable stock** (see pages 10 and 13)

pinch of **cayenne pepper**, or more to taste

salt

To garnish

2–3 tablespoons finely diced **dessert apple**

paprika

Melt the butter or margarine in a large saucepan and cook the celeriac and apples over a moderate heat for 5 minutes or until they have begun to soften.

Add the stock and cayenne pepper and bring to the boil. Reduce the heat, cover the pan and simmer for 15–20 minutes or until the celeriac and apples are very soft.

Purée the mixture in a blender or food processor until it is very smooth, transferring each batch to a clean saucepan. Alternatively, rub through a fine sieve. Reheat gently. Season to taste and serve in individual bowls, garnished with the finely diced apple and a dusting of paprika.

For celeriac & roasted garlic soup, halve 2 garlic bulbs, put into a roasting tin, drizzle with 2 teaspoons olive oil then roast in a preheated oven, 200°C (400°F), Gas Mark 6, for 15 minutes. Heat the butter in a saucepan as above, add the celeriac and 1 chopped onion in place of the apples, fry gently for 5 minutes. Take the garlic out of the papery skins, add to the celeriac with 1 litre (1¾ pints) of vegetable stock, salt and cayenne pepper. Simmer as above. Purée, reheat with 150 ml (¼ pint) milk then serve swirled with a little double cream in each bowl.

broccoli & almond soup

Serves **6**

Preparation time **15 minutes**

Cooking time **15 minutes**

25 g (1 oz) **butter**

1 **onion**, roughly chopped

500 g (1 lb) **broccoli**, cut into florets, stems sliced

40 g (1½ oz) **ground almonds**

900 ml (1½ pints) **vegetable** or **chicken stock** (see pages 13 and 10)

300 ml (½ pint) **milk**

salt and **pepper**

To garnish

15 g (½ oz) **butter**

6 tablespoons **natural yogurt**

3 tablespoons **flaked almonds**

Heat the butter in a saucepan, add the onion and fry gently for 5 minutes until just beginning to soften. Stir in the broccoli until coated in the butter then add the ground almonds, stock and a little salt and pepper.

Bring to the boil then cover and simmer for 10 minutes until the broccoli is just tender and still bright green. Leave to cool slightly, then purée in batches in a blender or food processor until finely speckled with green.

Pour the purée back into the saucepan and stir in the milk. Reheat then taste and adjust the seasoning if needed. Heat the 15 g (½ oz) butter in a frying pan, add the almonds and fry for a few minutes, stirring until golden. Ladle the soup into bowls, drizzle a spoonful of yogurt over each bowl, then sprinkle with almonds.

For broccoli & Stilton soup, omit the ground almonds and cook as above, adding 125 g (4 oz) de-rinded and crumbled Stilton cheese when reheating the soup. Stir until melted, then ladle into bowls and sprinkle with a little extra cheese and some coarsely crushed black pepper.

minestrone

Serves **4**
Preparation time **5 minutes**
Cooking time **23 minutes**

2 tablespoons **olive oil**
1 **onion**, chopped
1 **garlic clove**, crushed
2 **celery sticks**, chopped
1 **leek**, finely sliced
1 **carrot**, chopped
400 g (13 oz) can **chopped tomatoes**
600 ml (1 pint) **chicken** or **vegetable stock** (see pages 10 and 13)
1 **courgette**, diced
½ small **cabbage**, shredded
1 **bay leaf**
75 g (3 oz) **canned haricot beans**
75 g (3 oz) **dried spaghetti**, broken into small pieces, or small **pasta shapes**
1 tablespoon chopped **flat leaf parsley**
salt and **pepper**
grated **Parmesan cheese**, to serve

Heat the oil in a large saucepan. Add the onion, garlic, celery, leek and carrot and cook over a medium heat, stirring occasionally, for 5 minutes. Add the tomatoes, stock, courgette, cabbage, bay leaf and haricot beans. Bring to the boil, lower the heat and simmer for 10 minutes.

Add the pasta and season to taste. Stir well and cook for a further 8 minutes. Keep stirring because the soup may stick to the base of the pan. Just before serving, add the parsley and stir well. Ladle into individual bowls and serve with grated Parmesan.

For minestrone with rocket & basil pesto, make up the soup as above then ladle into bowls. Top with spoonfuls of pesto made by finely chopping 25 g (1 oz) rocket leaves and 25 g (1 oz) basil leaves, 1 garlic clove and 25 g (1 oz) pine nuts. Mix with 2 tablespoons freshly grated Parmesan, a little salt and pepper and 125 ml (4 fl oz) olive oil. Alternatively, put all the pesto ingredients into a liquidizer or food processor and whiz together.

cream of leek & pea soup

Serves **6**
Preparation time **15 minutes**
Cooking time **20 minutes**

2 tablespoons **olive oil**
375 g (12 oz) **leeks**, slit and
    well washed then thinly
    sliced
375 g (12 oz) **fresh shelled**
    or **frozen peas**
small bunch **mint**
900 ml (1½ pints) **vegetable**
    or **chicken stock** (see pages
    13 and 10)
150 g (5 oz) **full-fat**
    mascarpone cheese
grated rind of 1 small **lemon**
salt and **pepper**

To garnish
mint leaves (optional)
lemon rind curls (optional)

Heat the oil in a saucepan, add the leeks, toss in the oil then cover and fry gently for 10 minutes, stirring occasionally, until softened but not coloured. Mix in the peas and cook briefly.

Pour the stock into the pan, add a little salt and pepper then bring to the boil. Cover and simmer gently for 10 minutes.

Ladle half the soup into a blender or food processor, add all the mint and blend until smooth. Pour the purée back into the saucepan. Mix the mascarpone with half of the lemon rind, reserving the rest for a garnish. Spoon half the mixture into the soup, then reheat, stirring until the mascarpone has melted. Taste and adjust the seasoning if needed. Ladle the soup into bowls, top with spoonfuls of the remaining mascarpone and a sprinkling of the remaining lemon rind. Garnish with mint leaves and lemon rind curls, if liked.

For cream of leek, pea & watercress soup, use just 175 g (6 oz) peas and add a roughly chopped bunch of watercress. Simmer in 600 ml (1 pint) of stock then, instead of adding the mascarpone, stir in 150 ml (¼ pint) milk and 150 ml (¼ pint) double cream, drizzling a little extra cream over at the end and topping with some crispy grilled and chopped bacon to garnish.

chilli, bean & pepper soup

Serves **6**

Preparation time **20 minutes**

Cooking time **30 minutes**

2 tablespoons **sunflower oil**

1 large **onion**, finely chopped

4 **garlic cloves**, finely chopped

2 **red peppers**, cored, deseeded and diced

2 **red chillies**, deseeded and finely chopped

900 ml (1½ pints) **vegetable stock** (see page 13)

750 ml (1¼ pints) **tomato juice** or **passata**

1 tablespoon **tomato purée**

1 tablespoon **sun-dried tomato paste**

2 tablespoons **sweet chilli sauce**

400 g (13 oz) can **red kidney beans**, drained

2 tablespoons finely chopped **coriander**

salt and **pepper**

75 ml (3 fl oz) **soured cream**, plus extra for serving (optional)

Heat the oil in a large saucepan and fry the onion and garlic until soft but not coloured. Stir in the peppers and chillies and fry for a few minutes. Stir in the stock and tomato juice or passata, the tomato purée and paste, chilli sauce, kidney beans and coriander. Bring to the boil, cover the pan and simmer for 20 minutes.

Cool slightly, then purée in a blender or food processor until smooth. Alternatively, rub through a sieve. Return the soup to the pan and adjust the seasoning, adding a little extra chilli sauce if necessary. Bring to the boil and serve in individual bowls. Stir a little soured cream into each portion and serve with tortilla chips, extra soured cream and lime zest, if liked.

For chilli, aubergine & pepper soup, heat

2 tablespoons sunflower oil in a saucepan, add 1 diced aubergine along with the onion and garlic, fry until the aubergine is very lightly browned then add the peppers and chillies. Add 600 ml (1 pint) stock then the tomato juice, tomato purée, paste and chilli sauce. Omit the red kidney beans and add a small bunch of basil instead. Simmer then purée as above and adjust the consistency if needed with a little extra stock.

stracciatella

Serves **6**
Preparation time **5 minutes**
Cooking time **4–6 minutes**

1.2 litres (2 pints) **chicken stock** (see page 10)
4 **eggs**
25 g (1 oz) freshly grated **Parmesan cheese**, plus extra to serve
2 tablespoons **fresh white breadcrumbs**
¼ teaspoon **grated nutmeg**
salt and **pepper**
basil leaves

Pour the stock into a saucepan and bring to the boil. Reduce the heat and simmer for 2–3 minutes. Beat the eggs, Parmesan, breadcrumbs and nutmeg in a bowl and season generously. Gradually whisk 2 ladlefuls of hot stock into the eggs.

Reduce the heat under the saucepan then slowly stir the egg mixture into the stock until smooth, making sure that the temperature remains moderate, as the egg will curdle if the soup boils. Gently simmer for 2–3 minutes until piping hot.

Tear the basil leaves into pieces and add to the pan, then ladle the soup into bowls. Serve with extra Parmesan to grate over the soup to taste.

For egg drop soup, heat 1.2 litres (2 pints) of chicken stock as above, then add ½ teaspoon of caster sugar and 1 tablespoon of soy sauce. Beat 2 eggs together in a small bowl. Stir the stock with a fork in a circular motion, then drizzle the beaten egg through the prongs of the fork held high over the soup so that it sets in droplets in the swirling stock. Leave for a minute or two until the egg has set, then ladle into bowls. Garnish with sliced green spring-onion tops and a little chopped coriander or green chilli.

courgette soup with gremolata

Serves **6**
Preparation time **15 minutes**
Cooking time **25 minutes**

25 g (1 oz) **butter**
1 **onion**, finely chopped
250 g (8 oz) **courgette**, diced
1 **celery stick**, diced
2 **garlic cloves**, finely
   chopped
75 g (3 oz) **arborio rice**
1.2 litres (2 pints) **chicken** or
   vegetable stock (see pages
   10 and 13)
150 ml (¼ pint) **dry white**
   wine
2 **eggs**, beaten
4 tablespoons freshly grated
   Parmesan cheese
salt and **pepper**

Gremolata
small bunch of **basil**
small bunch of **parsley**
2 teaspoons **capers**
grated rind of 1 **lemon**

Heat the butter in a saucepan, add the onion and
fry gently for 5 minutes until softened. Stir in the
courgette, celery and garlic and fry briefly, then stir
in the rice.

Pour in the stock and wine, season with salt and
pepper and simmer for 15 minutes, stirring occasionally
until the rice is tender.

Take the pan off the heat and leave to cool slightly.
Beat the eggs and Parmesan together in a bowl, then
gradually mix in a ladleful of the hot stock. Pour this
mixture back into the saucepan and stir well. Heat
gently until the soup has thickened slightly but do not
boil or the eggs will scramble.

Chop all the gremolata ingredients finely and mix
together. Ladle the soup into bowls and sprinkle with
the gremolata.

For courgette, lemon & salmon soup, make up the
soup as above, adding 375 g (12 oz) salmon steak for
the last 10 minutes of the soup's cooking time. Lift out
and flake the fish into pieces discarding the skin and
any bones. Beat 2 eggs with the juice of ½ lemon in a
bowl, gradually mix in a ladleful of the hot soup then
stir back into the saucepan. Heat gently until the soup
is slightly thickened. Divide the salmon between
serving bowls, ladle the soup on top and sprinkle with
a little parsley.

pea, lettuce & lemon soup

Serves **4**
Preparation time **10 minutes**
Cooking time **15–20 minutes**

25 g (1 oz) **butter**
1 large **onion**, finely chopped
425 g (14 oz) **frozen peas**
2 **little gem lettuces**, roughly
  chopped
1 litre (1¾ pints) **vegetable** or
  chicken stock (see pages
  13 and 10)
grated rind and juice of
  ½ lemon
salt and **pepper**

Sesame croûtons
2 thick slices of **bread**, cubed
1 tablespoon **olive oil**
1 tablespoon **sesame seeds**

Brush the bread cubes with the oil and put in a roasting tin. Sprinkle with the sesame seeds and bake in a preheated oven, 200°C (400°F), Gas Mark 6, for 10–15 minutes, or until golden.

Meanwhile, heat the butter in a large saucepan and fry the onion for 5 minutes until softened. Add the peas, lettuce, stock, lemon rind and juice and salt and pepper to taste. Bring to the boil, then reduce the heat, cover the pan and simmer for 10–15 minutes.

Allow the soup to cool slightly, then transfer to a blender or food processor and whiz until smooth. Return the soup to the pan, adjust the seasoning if necessary and heat through. Spoon into warmed serving bowls and sprinkle with the sesame croûtons.

For pea, spinach & lemon soup, make up the soup as above adding 125 g (4 oz) young leaf spinach instead of the little gem lettuces. Simmer for 10–15 minutes then purée. Reheat and add a little grated nutmeg to taste. Ladle into bowls and top with 2 teaspoons natural yogurt per serving.

garden herb soup

Serves **4**
Preparation time **15 minutes**
Cooking time **30 minutes**

50 g (2 oz) **butter**
1 **onion**, roughly chopped
1 **baking potato**, about 250 g
   (8 oz), diced
1 litre (1¾ pints) **ham,
   chicken** or **vegetable stock**
   (see pages 10 and 13)
75 g (3 oz) **mixed parsley**
   and **chives**, roughly torn
   into pieces
salt and **pepper**

Heat the butter in a saucepan, add the onion and fry gently for 5 minutes until softened but not browned. Add the potato, toss in the butter then cover and fry gently for 10 minutes, stirring occasionally until just turning golden around the edges.

Add the stock, season with salt and pepper and bring to the boil. Cover and simmer for 10 minutes or until the potatoes are tender. Cool slightly then purée in batches in a blender or food processor with the herbs.

Pour back into the saucepan, reheat then taste and adjust the seasoning if needed. Serve in mugs with toasted bacon sandwiches.

For Italian herb soup, heat 2 tablespoons of olive oil in a pan, add the onion and fry until softened. Mix in 150 g (5 oz) diced potato, cover and fry for 10 minutes. Mix in the stock and seasoning as above, cover and simmer for 10 minutes. Purée the soup in the blender, replacing the parsley and chives with 75 g (3 oz) rocket leaves, and adding 25 g (1 oz) ground pine nuts or almonds and 40 g (1½ oz) freshly grated Parmesan. Reheat and serve topped with toasted pine nuts.

red chicken & coconut broth

Serves **4**
Preparation time **10 minutes**
Cooking time **20–21 minutes**

1 tablespoon **sunflower oil**
250 g (8 oz) boned and
  skinned **chicken thighs**,
  diced
4 teaspoons **ready-made red
  Thai curry paste**
1 teaspoon **ready-made
  galangal paste**
3 dried **kaffir lime leaves**
400 ml (13 fl oz) can **full-fat
  coconut milk**
2 teaspoons **Thai fish sauce**
1 teaspoon **light muscovado
  sugar**
600 ml (1 pint) **chicken stock**
  (see page 10)
4 **spring onions**, thinly sliced,
  plus 2 extra to garnish
50 g (2 oz) **mangetout**, sliced
100 g (3½ oz) **bean sprouts**,
  rinsed
small bunch of **coriander
  leaves**

Heat the oil in a saucepan, add the chicken and curry paste and fry for 3–4 minutes until just beginning to colour. Stir in the galangal paste, lime leaves, coconut milk, fish sauce and muscovado sugar, then mix in the stock.

Bring to the boil, cover and simmer for 15 minutes, stirring occasionally until the chicken is cooked.

Create curls by cutting very thin strips from the two spring onions reserved for a garnish. Soak in cold water for 10 minutes, then drain.

Add the remaining spring onions, mangetout and bean sprouts and cook for 2 minutes. Ladle into bowls and tear the coriander leaves over the top. Scatter the spring onion curls over the soup.

For red fish & coconut broth, heat the oil, add the curry paste and fry for 1 minute. Add the galangal paste, lime leaves, coconut milk, fish sauce and muscovado sugar. Pour in the stock then add a 250 g (8 oz) salmon fillet. Cover and simmer for 10 minutes, lift out the fish and flake it into pieces, discarding the skin and bones. Return the salmon to the broth, add the vegetables and 125 g (4 oz) small prawns, defrosted and rinsed if frozen. Cook for 2 minutes then serve with the coriander leaves as above.

prawn & noodle soup

Serves **4**

Preparation time **10 minutes**

Cooking time **15 minutes**

900 ml (1½ pints) **vegetable**
  or **chicken stock** (see pages
  13 and 10)

2 dried **kaffir lime leaves**

1 **lemon grass stalk**, lightly
  bruised

150 g (5 oz) **dried egg
  noodles**

50 g (2 oz) **frozen peas**

50 g (2 oz) **frozen sweetcorn**

100 g (3½ oz) large **king
  prawns**, cooked, peeled and
  deveined, or defrosted if
  frozen, rinsed with cold
  water and drained

4 **spring onions**, sliced

2 teaspoons **soy sauce**

Put the stock into a saucepan with the lime leaves and lemon grass, bring to the boil, then reduce the heat and simmer for 10 minutes.

Add the noodles to the stock and cook according to the packet instructions. After 2 minutes, add the peas, sweetcorn, prawns, spring onions and soy sauce and cook for 2 more minutes. Remove and discard the lemon grass. Serve the soup in warmed bowls.

For chicken & noodle soup, put the stock, lime leaves and lemon grass into a saucepan then add 2 boneless, skinless, chicken breasts that have been diced, bring to the boil then simmer for 10 minutes. Continue as above.

cream of sweetcorn soup

Serves **4–6**

Preparation time **5–10 minutes**

Cooking time about **25–30 minutes**

40 g (1½ oz) **butter**
1 **onion**, chopped
2 **potatoes**, diced
25 g (1 oz) **plain flour**
900 ml (1½ pints) **milk**
1 **bay leaf**
2 x 325 g (11 oz) cans **sweetcorn**, drained
6 tablespoons **double cream**
salt and **pepper**
fried **bacon**, crumbled, to garnish

Melt the butter in a large saucepan. Add the onion and potatoes and cook over a low heat, stirring frequently, for 5 minutes, without browning.

Stir in the flour, then gradually add the milk, stirring constantly. Bring to the boil, add the bay leaf and season to taste with salt and pepper. Add half the sweetcorn, cover the pan and simmer for 15–20 minutes.

Remove and discard the bay leaf and set the soup aside to cool slightly. Purée the soup in a blender or food processor or rub it through a sieve until smooth. Return it to the pan, add the remaining sweetcorn and heat through.

Stir in the cream, sprinkle over the bacon and serve the soup immediately.

For cream of sweet potato & sweetcorn soup, fry the onion in the butter as above, add 425 g (14 oz) diced sweet potato instead of the ordinary potatoes then continue as above. Serve the soup with a little diced and fried chorizo sausage instead of the bacon.

mediterranean garlic soup

Serves **4**

Preparation time **10 minutes**

Cooking time **16–18 minutes**

2 tablespoons **olive oil**

2–3 **garlic cloves**, finely
chopped

125 g (4 oz) **chorizo**, diced

6 tablespoons **red wine**

1 litre (1¾ pints) **beef stock**
(see page 12) or **game
stock**

2 teaspoons **tomato purée**

1 teaspoon **brown sugar**

4 **eggs**

salt and **pepper**

parsley, chopped, to garnish

Heat the oil in a saucepan, add the garlic and chorizo and fry gently for 3–4 minutes. Add the wine, stock, tomato purée and sugar, season with salt and pepper and simmer for 5 minutes.

Reduce the heat to a very gentle simmer then drop the eggs one at a time into the liquid, leaving space between them. Poach for 3–4 minutes until the whites are set and the yolks set to your liking.

Taste and adjust the seasoning if needed, then ladle an egg into the base of each serving bowl, cover with the soup and sprinkle with a little chopped parsley. Serve with diced croûtons (see page 15).

For garlic & potato soup, add 375 g (12 oz) diced potato when frying the onion and chorizo. Add the wine, stock, tomato purée, sugar and seasoning and simmer for 30 minutes. Ladle the soup into bowls and serve with garlic croûtes topped with grated Gruyère cheese (see page 226).

hot & sour soup

Serves **4**

Preparation time **10 minutes**

Cooking time **12 minutes**

750 ml (1¼ pints) **vegetable or fish stock** (see page 13)

4 dried **kaffir lime leaves**

2.5 cm (1 inch) piece **fresh root ginger**, peeled and grated

1 **red chilli**, deseeded and sliced

1 **lemon grass stalk**, lightly bruised

125 g (4 oz) **mushrooms**, sliced

100 g (3½ oz) **rice noodles**

75 g (3 oz) **baby spinach**

125 g (4 oz) cooked, peeled **tiger prawns**, or defrosted if frozen, rinsed with cold water and drained

2 tablespoons **lemon juice**

freshly ground **black pepper**

Put the stock, lime leaves, fresh root ginger, chilli and lemon grass in a large saucepan. Cover and bring to the boil. Add the mushrooms and simmer for 2 minutes. Break the noodles into short lengths, drop into the soup and simmer for 3 minutes.

Add the baby spinach and prawns and simmer for 2 minutes until the prawns are heated through. Add the lemon juice. Remove and discard the lemon grass stalk and season the soup with black pepper before serving.

For hot coconut soup, make up the soup as above, adding just 450 ml (¾ pint) stock and a 400 ml (14 fl oz) can coconut milk, plus 2 teaspoons ready-made Thai red curry paste. Continue as above and serve sprinkled with a little chopped coriander.

cheesy cauliflower & cider soup

Serves **6**
Preparation time **15 minutes**
Cooking time **30 minutes**

40 g (1½ oz) **butter**
1 **onion**, finely chopped
200 g (7 oz) **potato**, coarsely
    grated
1 **cauliflower**, cut into small
    florets, woody core
    discarded, about 500 g
    (1 lb) when prepared
900 ml (1½ pints) **chicken** or
    vegetable stock (see pages
    10 and 13)
300 ml (½ pint) **dry cider**
2 teaspoons **wholegrain**
    mustard
75 g (3 oz) **mature Cheddar**
    cheese, grated
salt and **cayenne pepper**
chopped chives, to garnish

Heat the butter in a saucepan, add the onion and fry gently for 5 minutes until just beginning to turn golden around the edges. Stir in the potato and cook briefly, then mix in the cauliflower florets, stock, cider and mustard. Season with salt and pepper and bring to the boil. Cover and simmer for 15 minutes until the vegetables are tender.

Mash the soup roughly to thicken it slightly, then stir in the cheese and heat, stirring until melted. Taste and adjust the seasoning if needed, then ladle into bowls. Garnish with chopped chives and serve with croûtons (see page 15) or Welsh rarebit toasts.

For Welsh rarebit toasts, to serve as an accompaniment, mix 125 g (4 oz) grated mature Cheddar with 1 egg yolk, 2 teaspoons Worcestershire sauce, 1 teaspoon wholegrain mustard and a little cayenne pepper. Toast 4 slices of bread lightly on both sides. Spread the cheese mixture over the top of each then cook under a hot grill until the cheese is bubbling and golden. Cut into thin strips to serve.

chilled
soups

beetroot & apple soup

Serves **6**
Preparation time **25 minutes**
Cooking time **50 minutes**,
  plus chilling

1 tablespoon **olive oil**
1 **onion**, roughly chopped
500 g (1 lb) bunch of
  uncooked **beetroot**,
  trimmed, peeled and diced
1 large **cooking apple**, about
  375 g (12 oz), quartered,
  cored, peeled and diced
1.5 litres (2½ pints) **vegetable**
  or **chicken stock** (see pages
  13 and 10)
salt and **pepper**

To finish
6 tablespoons **soured cream**
1 **red dessert apple**, cored
  and diced
seeds from ½ **pomegranate**
4 tablespoons **maple syrup**

Heat the oil in a saucepan, add the onion and fry gently for 5 minutes until softened. Add the beetroot and apple, pour in the stock, season with salt and pepper and bring to the boil. Cover and simmer for 45 minutes, stirring occasionally until the beetroot is tender.

Allow the soup to cool slightly, then purée in batches in a blender or food processor until smooth. Pour into a large jug, taste and adjust the seasoning if needed, then chill in the refrigerator for 3–4 hours or overnight.

Pour the soup into bowls to serve and top with a spoonful of soured cream, sprinkle with the diced apple and pomegranate seeds, then drizzle with a little maple syrup. Serve extra maple syrup in a small jug to add as required and accompany with sliced rye bread, if liked.

For beetroot & orange soup, fry the onion in oil as above, add the beetroot (omit the apple) and simmer with the stock and a little salt and pepper for 45 minutes. Purée the soup as above and mix with the grated rind and juice of 2 large oranges. Chill and serve with a swirl of cream, a drizzle of honey and some orange-rind curls made with a zester.

chillied melon foam

Serves **6**
Preparation time **15 minutes**

2 ripe **Galia melons**
freshly squeezed **juice of
  1 lime**
½–1 large **mild red chilli**,
  deseeded and quartered
small bunch of **coriander**, plus
  extra sprigs to garnish
300 ml (½ pint) pressed
  apple juice
lime wedges, to garnish
  (optional)

Cut the melons in half, scoop out and discard the seeds, then scoop the flesh away from the skin and put it into a blender or food processor with the lime juice, chilli and coriander, torn into pieces. Add half the apple juice and blend until smooth. Gradually mix in the remaining juice until frothy.

Pour the soup into cups or glass tumblers half filled with ice and serve immediately, garnished with a sprig of coriander and lime wedges if liked, before the foamy texture loses its bubbles.

For gingered melon foam, scoop out the flesh from 2 halved, deseeded, charentais melons, then purée with 2 chopped spring onions and 150 ml (¼ pint) low-fat crème fraîche in a blender or food processor. Add 150 ml (¼ pint) ginger beer and purée until frothy. Pour into shallow bowls or back into the empty melon shells to serve.

sour cherry soup

Serves **6**
Preparation time **10 minutes**
Cooking time **12 minutes**,
   plus chilling

300 ml (½ pint) **white riesling wine**
450 ml (¾ pint) **water**
2 tablespoons **caster sugar**
1 **cinnamon stick**, halved
grated **rind** and **juice** of
   1 **lemon**
475 g (15 oz) pack **frozen pitted cherries**
300 ml (½ pint) **soured cream**
ground cinnamon, to garnish

Pour the wine and water into a saucepan, add the sugar, cinnamon stick and lemon rind and juice. Bring to the boil and simmer for 5 minutes.

Add the still frozen cherries and simmer for 5 minutes. Discard the cinnamon stick, then ladle half the liquid and cherries into a blender or food processor. Add the soured cream and then blend, in batches if needed, until smooth. Return the blended liquid to the saucepan and mix well.

Chill the soup thoroughly, then ladle into shallow bowls so that the whole cherries can be seen and sprinkle with a little ground cinnamon to garnish. Serve with some cherries on stalks, if liked.

For peppered strawberry soup, make up the syrup as above with the wine, water, sugar and lemon rind and juice, adding ½ teaspoon crushed coloured peppercorns in place of the cinnamon. Simmer for 5 minutes then add 500 g (1 lb) sliced or halved strawberries depending on their size. Finish the soup as above.

avocado & soured cream soup

Serves **6**
Preparation time **15 minutes**
Cooking time **5 minutes**

1 tablespoon **sunflower oil**
4 **spring onions**, sliced, plus
   2 extra to garnish
2 large ripe **avocados**, halved
   and stoned
4 tablespoons **soured cream**
600 ml (1 pint) **vegetable** or
   chicken stock (see pages
   13 and 10)
juice of 2 **limes**
salt and **pepper**
Tabasco sauce

Heat the oil in a frying pan, add the spring onions and fry for 5 minutes until softened. Cut very thin strips from the remaining spring onions to create curls. Soak in cold water for 10 minutes, then drain.

Scoop out the avocado flesh from the shells with a dessertspoon and add to a blender or food processor with the fried spring onions, the soured cream and about a third of the stock. Blend until a smooth purée, then gradually mix in the remaining stock and lime juice. Season to taste with salt, pepper and a few drops of Tabasco sauce.

Serve the soup immediately while the avocado is still bright green in cups or glass tumblers containing some ice. Scatter the spring onion curls over the soup and serve with breadsticks or grissini.

For homemade salt & pepper grissini, to serve as an accompaniment, put 250 g (8 oz) strong white flour into a bowl and mix with ¼ teaspoon salt, 1 teaspoon caster sugar and 1 teaspoon fast-action dried yeast. Add 4 teaspoons olive oil and gradually mix in up to 150 ml (¼ pint) warm water until you've made a smooth dough. Knead for 5 minutes on a lightly floured surface, then cut the dough into 18 pieces and roll each into a thin rope. Put these on a greased baking sheet, cover with oiled clingfilm and leave in a warm place to rise for 30 minutes. Remove the clingfilm, brush the bread with beaten egg, then sprinkle with a little coarse sea salt and a generous scattering of roughly crushed black peppercorns. Bake in a preheated oven, 200°C (400°F), Gas Mark 6, for 6–8 minutes until golden. Serve warm or cold with the soup.

fennel vichyssoise

Serves **6**
Preparation time **20 minutes**
Cooking time **30 minutes**,
  plus chilling

25 g (1 oz) **butter**
1 **fennel bulb**, about
  200–250 g (7–8 oz), green
  feathery tops trimmed and
  reserved, core discarded,
  bulb roughly chopped
4 **spring onions**, thickly sliced
150 g (5 oz) **potato**, diced
450 ml (¾ pint) **chicken stock**
  (see page 10)
250 ml (8 fl oz) **milk**
150 ml (¼ pint) **double
  cream**
salt and **pepper**

Heat the butter in a saucepan, add the chopped fennel, spring onions and potato, toss in the butter then cover and fry gently for 10 minutes, stirring occasionally until softened but not browned.

Pour in the stock, season and bring to the boil. Cover and simmer for 15 minutes until the vegetables are just tender and still tinged green.

Allow the soup to cool slightly, then purée in batches in a blender or food processor until smooth. Pour the purée through a fine sieve back into the saucepan, then press the coarser pieces of fennel through the sieve using the back of a ladle. Mix in the milk and cream, then taste and adjust the seasoning if needed. Chill well.

Ladle the soup into small bowls or glasses half filled with ice and garnish with the reserved green feathery tops, snipped into small pieces.

For classic vichyssoise, omit the fennel and spring onions and add instead 375 g (12 oz) leeks that have been slit, rinsed well in cold water then drained and sliced. Stir half the cream into the soup and swirl the rest through the bowls before serving. Garnish with a sprinkling of a few snipped chives.

gazpacho

Serves **6**

Preparation time **10–15 minutes**, plus chilling

2 **garlic cloves**, roughly chopped

¼ teaspoon **salt**

3 slices of **thick white bread**, crusts removed

375 g (12 oz) **tomatoes**, skinned and coarsely chopped

½ large **cucumber**, peeled, deseeded and coarsely chopped

1 large **red pepper**, cored, deseeded and coarsely chopped

2 **celery sticks**, quartered

5 tablespoons **olive oil**

4 tablespoons **white wine vinegar**

1 litre (1¾ pints) **water**

freshly ground **black pepper**

To garnish

2 **tomatoes**, deseeded and diced

¼ **cucumber**, diced

½ **red onion**, finely chopped

Combine the chopped garlic and salt in a mortar and pound with a pestle until smooth. Alternatively, place the garlic and salt on a board and crush the garlic with the flattened blade of a knife. Place the bread in a bowl and cover with cold water. Soak for 5 seconds, then drain the bread and squeeze out the moisture.

Place the tomatoes, cucumber, pepper and celery in a blender or food processor. Add the garlic paste, bread and oil and purée the mixture until very smooth.

Pour the mixture into a large bowl and stir in the vinegar and water and add pepper to taste. Cover closely and chill in the refrigerator for at least 3 hours. Serve the soup very cold in individual chilled glasses. Garnish with a sprinkling of the diced tomatoes, cucumber and red onion.

For chilled gazpacho, make up the soup as above, adding 1 large, mild, deseeded and finely chopped red chilli along with the other vegetables. Serve garnished with a scattering of finely chopped mint and a drizzle of olive oil.

chilled almond & grape soup

Serves **6**

Preparation time **20 minutes**, plus chilling

100 g (3½ oz) stale **ciabatta bread**, crusts removed
600 ml (1 pint) **chicken stock** (see page 10)
100 g (3½ oz) **blanched almonds**
1–2 **garlic cloves**, sliced
2 tablespoons **olive oil**
2 tablespoons **sherry vinegar**
salt and **pepper**

To garnish
3 tablespoons **flaked almonds**, toasted
150 g (5 oz) **seedless grapes**, halved

Tear the bread into pieces into a bowl, pour over 150 ml (¼ pint) of the stock and leave to soak for 5 minutes until softened.

Grind the almonds and garlic together in a food processor or liquidizer until they form a fine powder then add the soaked bread with its stock, the oil, vinegar and a little salt and pepper. Blend together then gradually mix in the remaining stock.

Chill for at least 2 hours. Taste and adjust the seasoning if needed, then ladle into small bowls and sprinkle the grapes and flaked almonds to garnish. Serve with fresh ciabatta.

For chilled tomato & almond soup, make up the soup as above, soaking the bread in 150 ml (¼ pint) stock then mixing in 450 ml (¾ pint) extra stock along with 150 ml (¼ pint) passata. Chill well and garnish with toasted flaked almonds, 4 pieces sun-dried tomato in oil and some basil leaves in place of the grapes.

bloody mary soup

Serves **6**
Preparation time **20 minutes**
Cooking time **25 minutes**,
  plus chilling

1 tablespoon **olive oil**, plus
  extra to serve
1 **onion**, chopped
1 **red pepper**, cored,
  deseeded and diced
2 **celery sticks**, sliced
500 g (1 lb) **plum tomatoes**,
  chopped
900 ml (1½ pints) **vegetable
  stock** (see page 13)
2 teaspoons **caster sugar**
4 teaspoons **Worcestershire
  sauce**
4 teaspoons **tomato purée**
4 tablespoons **vodka**
few drops of **Tabasco sauce**
salt and **pepper**
baby **celery sticks with
  leaves**, to garnish

Heat the oil in a saucepan, add the onion and fry for
5 minutes until softened but not browned. Stir in the
red pepper, celery and tomatoes and fry for 5 minutes,
stirring occasionally.

Pour in the stock, add the sugar, Worcestershire sauce,
tomato purée and a little salt and pepper and bring to
the boil. Cover and simmer for 15 minutes.

Allow the soup to cool slightly, then purée in batches
in a blender or food processor until smooth. Sieve if
liked then pour back into the saucepan. Add the vodka
and Tabasco to taste, and adjust the seasoning
if needed. Chill well.

Ladle the soup into small bowls or glasses, add tiny
celery sticks, drizzle with a little extra olive oil and
sprinkle with a little extra pepper.

For virgin mary & pesto soup, fry the onion in the
oil as above, add the red pepper, celery and tomatoes,
then simmer in 900 ml (1½ pints) stock mixed with
4 teaspoons sun-dried tomato paste and 2 teaspoons
caster sugar for 15 minutes. Purée with 1 tablespoon
pesto. Chill and serve with a little extra pesto added to
each bowl and garnished with a few tiny basil leaves.

yogurt, walnut & cucumber soup

Serves **4**

Preparation time **15 minutes**,
  plus soaking and chilling

½ **cucumber**

25 g (1 oz) **walnut pieces**

1 **garlic clove**

4 stems **dill**

½ slice **white bread**, torn into
  pieces

2 tablespoons **olive oil**

400 g (13 oz) **low-fat natural
  yogurt**

4 tablespoons **cold water**

2 teaspoons **lemon juice**

salt and **pepper**

To garnish

little extra **olive oil**

few chopped **walnuts**

dill sprigs

Peel off half the cucumber skin, then roughly chop the cucumber. Put it on to a plate and sprinkle with a little salt. Set aside for 20 minutes.

Rinse the cucumber with cold water and drain well in a sieve. Put the walnuts, garlic, dill, bread and oil into a blender or food processor and whiz until finely chopped. Add the cucumber and yogurt and blend again until the cucumber is finely chopped. Mix in the water, lemon juice and season with salt and pepper to taste. Chill well.

Ladle into glasses. Drizzle the top with a little extra olive oil, sprinkle on a few walnuts and a sprig or two of dill. Serve with strips of toasted pitta bread, if liked.

For minted yogurt, almond & cucumber soup, salt the cucumber as above. Omit the walnuts, garlic and dill, adding 25 g (1 oz) ground almonds and 2 stems fresh mint in their place. Blend with the bread and oil as above, then add the rinsed and drained cucumber, yogurt, water, lemon juice and season with salt and pepper. Blend again, then chill. Ladle into bowls and garnish with a swirl of olive oil, a few toasted flaked almonds and some tiny mint leaves.

chilled lettuce soup

Serves **6**
Preparation time **15 minutes**
Cooking time **14–15 minutes**,
  plus chilling

25 g (1 oz) **butter**
4 **spring onions**, sliced
250 g (8 oz) **shelled fresh** or
  frozen peas
1 **Romaine lettuce heart**,
  leaves separated, rinsed
600 ml (1 pint) **chicken** or
  vegetable stock (see pages
  10 and 13)
1 teaspoon **caster sugar**
6 tablespoons **double cream**
salt and **pepper**

To serve
12 **Little Gem lettuce leaves**
1 small fresh prepared
  crab on the shell, about
  150 g (5 oz)
2 tablespoons **mayonnaise**
1 tablespoon **lemon juice**
a little **paprika**

Heat the butter in a saucepan, add the spring onions and fry for 2–3 minutes until softened. Add the peas, cook for 2 minutes then shred and add the lettuce. Pour over the stock, add the sugar and a little salt and pepper and bring to the boil.

Cover and simmer gently for 10 minutes until the lettuce is wilted but still bright green. Allow to cool slightly, then purée in batches in a blender or food processor until smooth. Stir in the cream, then taste and adjust the seasoning if needed. Chill well.

Ladle the soup into small bowls set on plates. Serve with Little Gem lettuce leaves topped with a small amount of crab mixed with the mayonnaise and lemon juice and sprinkled with paprika.

For chilled watercress soup, heat the butter as above, slice 1 small leek, add the white slices and 200 g (7 oz) diced potato, cover and fry gently for 10 minutes, stirring occasionally. Add 750 ml (1¼ pints) chicken or vegetable stock, season then cover and simmer for 10 minutes. Add the green leek tops, 2 bunches or 200 g (7 oz) watercress, cover and cook for 5 minutes until the watercress is just wilted. Purée in batches as above, then return to the pan and mix with 150 ml (¼ pint) milk and 150 ml (¼ pint) double cream. Chill well. Serve in shallow bowls with a swirl of cream.

winter warmers

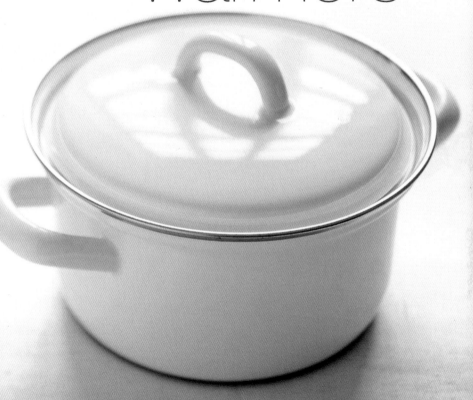

smoked aubergine & tomato soup

Serves **6**
Preparation time **20 minutes**
Cooking time **60 minutes**

2 large **aubergines**
2 tablespoons **olive oil**
1 large **onion**, roughly
   chopped
2 **garlic cloves**, finely
   chopped
500 g (1 lb) **plum tomatoes**,
   skinned and chopped
½ teaspoon **smoked paprika**
1 teaspoon **caster sugar**
600 ml (1 pint) **vegetable** or
   chicken stock (see pages
   13 and 10)
salt and **pepper**

Anchovy toasts
50 g (2 oz) can **anchovy**
   fillets in oil, drained, finely
   chopped
2 tablespoons **chopped**
   chives
75 g (3 oz) **butter**
1 small **baguette** or ½ **French**
   stick, sliced

Prick each aubergine just below the stalk and cook under a hot grill for 15 minutes, turning several times until the skin is blistered and blackened. Transfer to a chopping board and leave to cool.

Heat the oil in a large saucepan, add the onion and fry, stirring for 5 minutes until softened. Meanwhile, cut the aubergines in half and use a spoon to scoop out the soft flesh, leaving the blackened skin behind.

Add the aubergine flesh and garlic to the onion and fry for 2 minutes. Mix in the tomatoes, smoked paprika and sugar and cook briefly, then stir in the stock and season with salt and pepper. Bring to the boil, cover and simmer for 30 minutes.

Purée the soup in batches in a blender or food processor until smooth. Pour back into the saucepan and reheat. Mix together the anchovies, chives, butter and a little pepper. Toast the bread and spread with the anchovy butter. Ladle the soup into bowls and float the anchovy toasts on top. Serve immediately.

For smoked tomato soup, omit the aubergines and add 875 g (1¾ lb) skinned and chopped tomatoes to the fried onion and garlic. Flavour with smoked paprika as above then simmer with the stock, sugar and salt and pepper. Serve the puréed soup with a drizzle of chillied olive oil instead of the anchovy toasts.

spiced lamb & sweet potato soup

Serves **6**
Preparation time **30 minutes**
Cooking time **2½ hours**

1 tablespoon **olive oil**
500 g (1 lb) **stewing lamb on the bone**
1 **onion**, finely chopped
1–2 **garlic cloves**, finely chopped
2 teaspoons **ras el hanout Moroccan spice blend**
2.5 cm (1 inch) piece **fresh root ginger**, grated
2 litres (3½ pints) **lamb** or **chicken stock** (see pages 12 and 10)
75 g (3 oz) **red lentils**
300 g (10 oz) **sweet potato**, diced
175 g (6 oz) **carrot**, diced
salt and **pepper**
small bunch of **coriander**, to garnish (optional)

Heat the oil in a large saucepan, add the lamb and fry until browned on one side, turn it over and add the onion. Cook until the lamb is browned all over and the onion just beginning to colour.

Stir in the garlic, spice blend and ginger, then the stock, lentils and salt and pepper. Bring to the boil then reduce the heat, cover and simmer for 1½ hours.

Add the sweet potato and carrot, bring back to a simmer then re-cover and cook for 1 hour. Lift the lamb out of the soup with a draining spoon, put on to a plate then carefully remove bones and excess fat, breaking the meat into small pieces. Return the meat to the pan and reheat if needed. Taste and adjust the seasoning if needed.

Ladle the soup into bowls, sprinkle with torn coriander leaves and serve with hot fennel flat breads.

For homemade fennel flat breads, to serve as an accompaniment, put 200 g (7 oz) self-raising flour and ½ teaspoon baking powder into a bowl. Add 1 teaspoon fennel seeds that have been roughly crushed using a pestle and mortar and a little salt and pepper. Add 2 tablespoons olive oil, then gradually mix in 6–7 tablespoons of water to make a soft dough. Cut the dough into 6 pieces, then roll each piece out on a lightly floured surface until a rough oval shape about the size of a hand . Cook on a preheated ridged frying pan for 3–4 minutes each side until singed and puffy.

beef & barley brö

Serves **6**
Preparation time **20 minutes**
Cooking time **2 hours**

25 g (1 oz) **butter**
250 g (8 oz) **braising beef**,
   fat trimmed away and meat
   cut into small cubes
1 large **onion**, finely chopped
200 g (7 oz) **swede**, diced
150 g (5 oz) **carrot**, diced
100 g (3½ oz) **pearl barley**
2 litres (3½ pints) **beef stock**
   (see page 12)
2 teaspoons **dry English**
   mustard (optional)
salt and **pepper**
chopped **parsley**, to garnish

Heat the butter in a large saucepan, add the beef and onion and fry for 5 minutes, stirring, until the beef is browned and the onion just beginning to colour.

Stir in the diced vegetables, pearl barley, stock and mustard, if using. Season with salt and pepper and bring to the boil. Cover and simmer for 1¾ hours, stirring occasionally until the meat and vegetables are very tender. Taste and adjust the seasoning if needed. Ladle the soup into bowls and sprinkle with a little chopped parsley. Serve with warm potato bannocks or farls.

For lamb & barley hotchpot, substitute the beef for 250 g (8 oz) diced lamb fillet and fry with the onion as above. Add the sliced white part of 1 leek, 175 g (6 oz) each of diced swede, carrot and potato, then mix in 50 g (2 oz) pearl barley, 2 litres (3½ pints) lamb stock, 2–3 sprigs of rosemary and salt and pepper. Bring to the boil then cover and simmer for 1¾ hours. Discard the rosemary, add the remaining thinly sliced green leek and cook for 10 minutes. Ladle into bowls and sprinkle with a little extra chopped rosemary to serve.

cock-a-leekie soup

Serves **6**
Preparation time **30 minutes**
Cooking time **2 hours**

1 tablespoon **sunflower oil**
2 **chicken thigh** and **leg joints**, about 375 g (12 oz)
500 g (1 lb) **leeks**, thinly sliced, white and green parts kept separate
3 **smoked streaky bacon rashers**, diced
2.5 litres (4 pints) **chicken stock** (see page 10)
75 g (3 oz) **stoned prunes**, quartered
1 **bay leaf**
1 large **thyme sprig**
50 g (2 oz) **long-grain rice**
salt and **pepper**

Heat the oil in a large saucepan, add the chicken joints and fry on one side until golden. Turn them over and add the white sliced leeks and bacon. Fry until the chicken is golden all over and the leeks and bacon just beginning to colour.

Pour in the stock, then add the prunes, bay leaf and thyme, season with salt and pepper and bring to the boil. Cover and simmer for 1½ hours, stirring occasionally until the chicken is falling off the bones.

Lift the chicken, bay leaf and thyme sprigs out of the soup with a slotted spoon and put on to a plate. Remove the skin and bones from the chicken then cut the meat into pieces. Return the chicken to the pan, adding the rice and green leek slices. Simmer for 10 minutes until the rice and leeks are tender.

Taste and adjust the seasoning if needed. Ladle the soup into bowls and serve with warm, crusty bread.

For cream of chicken soup, omit the prunes and rice and use only 2 litres (3½ pints) stock. Add 250 g (8 oz) diced potato then bring to the boil and simmer for 1½ hours. Discard the herbs and purée the soup in batches in a blender or food processor. Stir in 150 ml (¼ pint) milk and 150 ml (¼ pint) double cream. Reheat and serve with croûtons (see page 15).

spring vegetable broth

Serves **4**

Preparation time **15 minutes**

Cooking time **30–35 minutes**

2 teaspoons **olive oil**

2 **celery sticks** with their
leaves, chopped

2 **leeks**, chopped

1 **carrot**, finely diced

50 g (2 oz) **pearl barley**

1.2 litres (2 pints) **vegetable
stock** (see page 13)

1 teaspoon **English mustard**

125 g (4 oz) **mangetout**,
sliced diagonally (optional)

salt and **pepper**

Heat the oil in a saucepan and add the celery, leeks
and carrot. Cook over a medium heat for 5 minutes.

Stir in the pearl barley, stock and mustard, season to
taste and simmer for 20–25 minutes. Add the
mangetout, if liked, and simmer for 5 minutes.

Ladle into warmed soup bowls and serve piping hot.

For winter vegetable broth, make up the soup
as above using just 1 chopped leek and adding
125 g (4 oz) finely diced swede. Simmer for
20 minutes then add 125 g (4 oz) finely shredded
green cabbage instead of the mangetout. Simmer for
10 minutes then ladle into bowls and top with diced
crispy grilled bacon.

onion, tomato & chickpea soup

Serves **6**
Preparation time **15 minutes**
Cooking time **1 hour 10
  minutes**

2 tablespoons **olive oil**
2 **red onions**, roughly
  chopped
2 **garlic cloves**, finely
  chopped
2 teaspoons **brown sugar**
625 g (1¼ lb) **tomatoes**,
  skinned if liked, roughly
  chopped
2 teaspoons **harissa paste**
3 teaspoons **tomato purée**
400 g (13 oz) can **chickpeas**,
  drained
900 ml (1½ pints) **vegetable**
  or **chicken stock** (see pages
  13 and 10)
salt and **pepper**

Heat the oil in a large saucepan, add the onions and fry
over a low heat for 10 minutes, stirring occasionally until
just beginning to brown around the edges. Stir in the
garlic and sugar and cook for 10 more minutes, stirring
more frequently as the onions begin to caramelize.

Stir in the tomatoes and harissa paste and fry for
5 minutes. Mix in the tomato purée, chickpeas, stock
and salt and pepper and bring to the boil. Cover and
simmer for 45 minutes until the tomatoes and onion are
very soft. Taste and adjust the seasoning if needed.

Ladle into bowls and serve with warm tomato ciabatta.

For chillied red onion & bean soup, make up
the soup as above but omit the harissa and add
1 teaspoon of smoked paprika and 1 split dried
red chilli when frying the tomatoes, then swap the
chickpeas for the same size can of red kidney beans.
Serve with garlic bread.

veg soup with bacon dumplings

Serves **6**

Preparation time **30 minutes**

Cooking time **1¼ – 1½ hours**

50 g (2 oz) **butter**

1 **onion**, finely chopped

1 **leek**, diced, white and green parts kept separate

300 g (10 oz) **swede**, diced

300 g (10 oz) **parsnip**, diced

300 g (10 oz) **carrot**, diced

2 **celery sticks**, diced

3–4 **sage** stems

2.5 litres (4 pints) **chicken stock** (see page 10)

salt and **pepper**

Dumplings

100 g (3½ oz) **self-raising flour**

½ teaspoon **English mustard powder**

2 teaspoons finely chopped **sage**

50 g (2 oz) **vegetable suet**

2 **smoked streaky bacon rashers**, finely chopped

4 tablespoons **water**

Heat the butter in a large saucepan, add the onion and white diced leeks and fry for 5 minutes until just beginning to soften. Add the other diced vegetables and sage, toss in the butter then cover and fry for 10 minutes, stirring occasionally.

Pour on the stock, season with salt and pepper and bring to the boil. Cover and simmer for 45 minutes, stirring occasionally until the vegetables are tender. Remove the sage then taste and adjust the seasoning if needed.

Make the dumplings by mixing the flour, mustard powder, sage, suet and bacon in a bowl with a little salt and pepper. Gradually stir in the water and mix first with a spoon, then squeeze together with your hands to make a smooth dough. Cut into 18 slices and roll each slice into a into small ball.

Stir the remaining green diced leek into the soup. Add the dumplings to the simmering soup, re-cover the pan and cook for 10 minutes until the dumplings are light and fluffy. Ladle into bowls and serve immediately.

For creamy winter vegetable soup, omit the dumplings and reduce the amount of stock to 1.5 litres (3 pints). Simmer for 45 minutes then purée in batches in a blender or food processor. Pour back into the saucepan, stir in 300 ml (½ pint) milk and reheat. Ladle into bowls, swirl 2 tablespoons of double cream into each portion and garnish with a little chopped sage and some crispy diced bacon.

christmas special

Serves **6**
Preparation **25 minutes**
Cooking time **about 1 hour**

25 g (1 oz) **butter**
1 **onion**, roughly chopped
2 **smoked streaky bacon rashers**, diced
250 g (8 oz) **potato**, diced
1 litre (1¾ pints) **chicken** or **turkey stock** (see page 10)
100 g (3½ oz) **vacuum-packed peeled chestnuts**
large pinch of **grated nutmeg**
250 g (8 oz) **Brussels sprouts**, sliced
salt and **pepper**
4 **smoked streaky bacon rashers**, grilled and diced, to garnish

Heat the butter in a saucepan, add the onion and fry gently for 5 minutes until softened. Add the bacon and potato, toss in the butter then cover and fry for 5 minutes until just beginning to brown.

Pour on the stock, crumble in the chestnuts, then add the nutmeg and salt and pepper. Bring to the boil, then cover and simmer for 30 minutes. Add the sliced sprouts and mix into the stock, then cover and simmer for 5 minutes until they are tender but still bright green.

Allow the soup to cool slightly, reserve a few sprout slices for the garnish, then purée it in batches in a blender or food processor until green specks can still be seen. Pour back into the saucepan and reheat. Taste and adjust the seasoning if needed. Garnish with the remaining Brussels sprouts and bacon.

For chestnut & mushroom soup, omit the Brussels sprouts and add 250 g (8 oz) sliced cup mushrooms after frying the potatoes and bacon and cook for 2–3 minutes, stirring frequently. Add the stock, chestnuts, nutmeg and salt and pepper, then bring to the boil and cook for 30 minutes. Purée and reheat the soup and serve garnished with cream, bacon and chestnuts as above.

harira

Serves **8–10**

Preparation time **about 25 minutes, plus soaking**

Cooking time **about 3 hours**

250 g (8 oz) **chickpeas,** soaked in cold water overnight

2 **chicken breasts,** halved

1.2 litres (2 pints) **chicken stock** (see page 10)

1.2 litres (2 pints) **water**

2 x 400 g (13 oz) cans **chopped tomatoes**

¼ teaspoon crumbled **saffron threads** (optional)

2 **onions,** chopped

125 g (4 oz) **long-grain rice**

50 g (2 oz) **green lentils**

2 tablespoons finely chopped **coriander**

2 tablespoons finely chopped **parsley**

salt and **pepper**

To garnish
natural yogurt
coriander sprigs

Drain the chickpeas, rinse under cold running water and drain again. Place them in a saucepan, cover with 5 cm (2 inches) of water and bring to the boil. Boil rapidly for 10 minutes, then lower the heat and simmer, partially covered, until tender, adding more water as necessary. This will take anything up to 1¾ hours. Drain the chickpeas and set aside.

Place the chicken breasts, stock and water in a second saucepan. Bring to the boil, lower the heat, cover the pan and simmer for 10–15 minutes or until the chicken is just cooked. Remove the chicken from the stock, place it on a board and shred it, discarding the skin.

Set the shredded chicken aside. Add the chickpeas, tomatoes, saffron (if using), onions, rice and lentils to the stock remaining in the pan. Cover the pan and simmer for 30–35 minutes or until the rice and lentils are tender.

Add the shredded chicken, coriander and parsley just before serving. Heat the soup for a further 5 minutes without letting it boil. Season to taste and serve the soup, garnished with drizzles of natural yogurt and coriander sprigs.

For budget harira, make up the soup as above omitting the chicken breasts and saffron, adding ½ teaspoon ground turmeric and ½ teaspoon ground cinnamon instead.

thai squash & coriander soup

Serves **6**
Preparation time **25 minutes**
Cooking time **51 minutes**

1 tablespoon **sunflower oil**
1 **onion**, roughly chopped
3 teaspoons **ready-made red Thai curry paste**
1–2 **garlic cloves**, finely chopped
2.5 cm (1 inch) piece of **fresh root ginger**, peeled and finely chopped
1 **butternut squash**, about 750 g (1½ lb), halved, deseeded, peeled and diced
400 ml (14 fl oz) can **full-fat coconut milk**
750 ml (1¼ pints) **vegetable** or **chicken stock** (see pages 13 and 10)
2 teaspoons **Thai fish sauce**
pepper
small bunch of **coriander**

Heat the oil in a saucepan, add the onion and fry gently for 5 minutes until softened. Stir in the curry paste, garlic and ginger and cook for 1 minute. Then mix in the squash, coconut milk, stock and fish sauce. Add a little pepper (don't add salt as the fish sauce is so salty) then bring to the boil.

Cover the pan and simmer for 45 minutes, stirring occasionally, until the squash is soft. Leave to cool slightly. Reserve a few sprigs of coriander for garnish then tear the remainder into pieces and add to the soup. Purée the soup in batches in a blender or food processor until smooth. Pour back into the saucepan and reheat, tearing in the reserved coriander sprigs. Ladle into bowls and serve.

For gingered squash soup, omit the Thai curry paste, coconut milk, fish sauce and coriander. Fry the onion as above then mix in the garlic and a 3.5 cm (1½ inch) piece of peeled and finely chopped fresh root ginger. Add the squash as above, 900 ml (1½ pints) of stock and a little salt and pepper, then bring to the boil. Cover and simmer for 45 minutes then purée and mix with 300 ml (½ pint) milk. Reheat and serve with croûtons (see page 15).

red pepper soup & pesto stifato

Serves **6**
Preparation time **30 minutes**
Cooking time **about 1 hour**

4 **red peppers**, halved, cored
and deseeded
3 tablespoons **olive oil**
1 large **onion**, roughly
chopped
2–3 **garlic cloves**, finely
chopped
400 g (13 oz) can **chopped
tomatoes**
900 ml (1½ pints) **vegetable**
or **chicken stock** (see pages
13 and 10)
2 tablespoons **balsamic
vinegar**
salt and **pepper**

To garnish
olive oil
handful of **basil leaves**
black pepper

Pesto stifato
2 **stifato sticks**, or long thin
bread rolls
2 tablespoons **pesto**
50 g (2 oz) **Parmesan
cheese**, grated

Arrange the peppers skin-side uppermost in a foil-lined grill pan, brush with 2 tablespoons of the oil, then grill for about 10 minutes until the skins are blackened and the peppers softened. Wrap the foil around the peppers, then leave them to cool for 10 minutes.

Meanwhile, heat the remaining oil in a saucepan, add the onion and fry gently for 5 minutes until softened and just beginning to brown. Mix in the garlic and cook for 1 minute, then mix in the tomatoes, stock, vinegar and salt and pepper.

Peel the blackened skins off the peppers then roughly chop the peppers. Add to the saucepan then bring to the boil, cover and simmer for 30 minutes. Allow to cool slightly, then purée in batches in a blender or food processor until smooth.

Return the soup to the pan, reheat then taste and adjust the seasoning if needed. Cut the stifato sticks or bread rolls into long strips, then lightly toast on both sides. Spread with the pesto then sprinkle with the cheese and grill until just melting. Ladle the soup into bowls and drizzle with some olive oil, a few basil leaves and some black pepper.

For roasted red pepper & cannellini bean soup,
grill the peppers as above. Skin and finely chop the peppers, then add to the fried onion, tomato and stock mixture. Omit the balsamic vinegar and add 3 large pinches of saffron threads and a drained 410 g (13½ oz) can cannellini beans. Season then cover and simmer for 30 minutes. Do not purée, but serve the soup chunky with garlic bread.

beef & noodle broth

Serves **2**
Preparation time **15 minutes**
Cooking time **15 minutes**

300 g (10 oz) **rump** or **sirloin
  steak**
2.5 cm (1 inch) piece of **fresh
  root ginger**, grated
2 teaspoons **soy sauce**
50 g (2 oz) **vermicelli rice
  noodles**
600 ml (1 pint) **beef** or
  chicken stock (see pages
  12 and 10)
1 **red chilli**, deseeded and
  finely chopped
1 **garlic clove**, thinly sliced
2 teaspoons **caster sugar**
2 teaspoons **vegetable oil**
75 g (3 oz) **sugar snap peas**,
  halved lengthways
small handful of **Thai basil**,
  torn into pieces

Trim any fat from the beef. Mix the ginger with
1 teaspoon of the soy sauce and smooth over both
sides of the beef. Cook the noodles according to the
directions on the packet. Drain and rinse thoroughly
in cold water.

Bring the stock to a gentle simmer with the chilli, garlic
and sugar. Cover and cook gently for 5 minutes.

Heat the oil in a small, heavy-based frying pan and fry
the beef for 2 minutes on each side. Transfer the meat
to a board, cut it in half lengthways and then cut it
across into thin strips.

Add the noodles, sugar snap peas, basil and remaining
soy sauce to the soup and heat gently for 1 minute.
Stir in the beef and serve immediately.

For minted chicken broth, replace the steak with the
same weight of boneless, skinless chicken breasts
and use chicken stock instead of beef. Make the soup
as above, but fry the chicken for 5–6 minutes on each
side until thoroughly cooked. Garnish the soup with a
small bunch of torn mint.

squash, kale & mixed bean soup

Serves **6**
Preparation time **15 minutes**
Cooking time **45 minutes**

1 tablespoon **olive oil**
1 **onion**, finely chopped
2 **garlic cloves**, finely
chopped
1 teaspoon **smoked paprika**
500 g (1 lb) **butternut
squash**, sliced, deseeded,
peeled and diced
2 small **carrots**, diced
500 g (1 lb) **tomatoes**,
skinned optional, roughly
chopped
410 g (13½ oz) can **mixed
beans**, drained
900 ml (1½ pints) **vegetable**
or **chicken stock** (see pages
13 and 10)
150 ml (¼ pint) **full-fat crème
fraîche**
100 g (3½ oz) **kale**, torn into
bite-sized pieces
salt and **pepper**

Heat the oil in a saucepan, add the onion and fry gently for 5 minutes. Stir in the garlic and smoked paprika and cook briefly, then add the squash, carrots, tomatoes and drained beans.

Pour on the stock, season with salt and pepper and bring to the boil, stirring. Cover and simmer for 25 minutes until the vegetables are tender.

Stir the crème fraîche into the soup, then add the kale, pressing it just beneath the surface of the stock. Cover and cook for 5 minutes until the kale has just wilted. Ladle into bowls and serve with warm garlic bread.

For cheesy squash, pepper & mixed bean soup,

fry the onion in oil as above, add the garlic, smoked paprika, squash, tomatoes and beans, adding a deseeded and diced red pepper instead of the carrot. Pour on the stock, then add 65 g (2½ oz) Parmesan rinds and season. Cover and simmer for 25 minutes. Stir in the crème fraîche but omit the kale. Discard the Parmesan rinds, ladle the soup into bowls and top with freshly grated Parmesan.

butternut squash & rosemary soup

Serves **4**

Preparation time **15 minutes**

Cooking time **1¼ hours**

1 **butternut squash**

2 tablespoons **olive oil**

a few **rosemary sprigs**, plus
extra to garnish

150 g (5 oz) **red lentils**,
washed

1 **onion**, finely chopped

900 ml (1½ pints) **vegetable
stock** (see page 13)

salt and **pepper**

Cut the squash in half and use a spoon to scoop out the seeds and fibrous flesh. Peel and cut the squash into small chunks and place in a roasting tin. Sprinkle over the oil and rosemary, and season well with salt and pepper. Roast in a preheated oven, 200°C (400°F), Gas Mark 6, for 45 minutes.

Meanwhile, place the lentils in a saucepan, cover with water, bring to the boil and boil rapidly for 10 minutes. Strain, then return the lentils to a clean saucepan with the onion and stock and simmer for 5 minutes. Season to taste.

Remove the squash from the oven, mash the flesh with a fork and add to the soup. Simmer for 25 minutes and then ladle into bowls. Garnish with more rosemary before serving.

For Indian spiced butternut squash soup, roast the squash and cook the lentils as above then drain. Heat 1 tablespoon sunflower oil in a saucepan, add 1 chopped onion and fry for 5 minutes until softened. Stir in 2 teaspoons mild curry paste and a 3.5 cm (1½ inch) piece of fresh root ginger, finely chopped. Add the drained lentils and stock and simmer for 5 minutes. Mash the squash as above and stir into the soup. Garnish with torn coriander leaves.

honey-roasted parsnip soup

Serves **6**
Preparation time **20 minutes**
Cooking time **50–55 minutes**

750 g (1½ lb) **parsnips**, cut
   into wedges
2 **onions**, cut into wedges
2 tablespoons **olive oil**
2 tablespoons **clear honey**
1 teaspoon **ground turmeric**
½ teaspoon **dried crushed
   chillies**
3 **garlic cloves**, thickly sliced
1.2 litres (2 pints) **vegetable**
   or **chicken stock** (see pages
   13 and 10)
2 tablespoons **sherry** or **cider
   vinegar**
150 ml (¼ pint) **double
   cream**
5 cm (2 inch) piece of **fresh
   root ginger**, peeled and
   grated
salt and **pepper**
a little **turmeric**, to garnish

Arrange the parsnips and onions in a large roasting tin in a single layer, then drizzle with the oil and honey. Sprinkle with the turmeric, crushed chillies and garlic.

Roast in a preheated oven, 190°C (375°F), Gas Mark 5, for 45–50 minutes, turning once until a deep golden brown with sticky, caramelized edges.

Transfer the roasting tin to the hob, add the stock, vinegar and salt and pepper and bring to the boil, scraping up the juices from the base of the pan. Simmer for 5 minutes.

Allow the soup to cool slightly, then purée in batches in a blender or food processor until smooth. Pour into a saucepan and reheat. Taste and adjust the seasoning and top up with a little extra stock, if needed. Mix the cream, ginger and a little pepper together. Ladle the soup into bowls and drizzle the ginger cream over the top, then garnish with a little turmeric, if liked. Serve with croûtons (see page 15).

For honey-roasted sweet potato soup, replace the parsnips with 750 g (1½ lb) sweet potato, cut into wedges, sprinkle with 1 teaspoon roughly crushed cumin seeds in addition to the turmeric and chilli, and roast and finish as above. Serve ladled into soup bowls topped with spoonfuls of natural yogurt and a teaspoon of mango chutney drizzled over each bowl.

split pea & parsnip soup

Serves **6**
Preparation time **20 minutes**
Cooking time **1¼ hours**

250 g (8 oz) **yellow split peas**, soaked overnight in cold water
300 g (10 oz) **parsnips**, cut into chunks
1 **onion**, roughly chopped
1.5 litres (2½ pints) **chicken or vegetable stock** (see pages 10 and 13)
salt and **pepper**

Coriander butter
1 teaspoon **cumin seeds**, roughly crushed
1 teaspoon **coriander seeds**, roughly crushed
2 **garlic cloves**, finely chopped
75 g (3 oz) **butter**
small bunch of **coriander**

Drain the soaked split peas and put them into a saucepan with the parsnips, onion and stock. Bring to the boil and boil for 10 minutes. Reduce the heat, cover and simmer for 1 hour or until the split peas are soft.

Meanwhile, make the butter by dry-frying the cumin and coriander seeds and garlic in a small saucepan until lightly toasted. Mix into the butter with the coriander leaves and a little salt and pepper. Shape into a sausage shape on clingfilm or foil, wrap up and chill until needed.

Roughly mash the soup or purée in batches in a liquidizer or food processor, if preferred. Reheat and stir in half the coriander butter until melted. Add a little extra stock if needed then season to taste. Ladle into bowls and top each bowl with a slice of the coriander butter. Serve with toasted pitta breads.

For split pea & carrot soup with chilli butter, make up the soup with 300 g (10 oz) diced carrots in place of the parsnips. Purée and reheat as above. Make a chilli butter by mixing 75 g (3 oz) butter with the grated rind and juice of 1 lime, 2 chopped spring onions and ½–1 large mild and finely chopped red chilli to taste.

beer broth with mini meatballs

Serves **6**
Preparation time **25 minutes**
Cooking time **about 1¼ hours**

25 g (1 oz) **butter**
1 **onion**, chopped
200 g (7 oz) **potato**, diced
125 g (4 oz) **swede** or
  parsnip, diced
1 **carrot**, diced
2 **tomatoes**, skinned if liked,
  roughly chopped
½ **lemon**, sliced
900 ml (1½ pints) **beef stock**
  (see page 12)
450 ml (¾ pint) can **lager**
¼ teaspoon **ground
  cinnamon**
¼ teaspoon **grated nutmeg**
100 g (3½ oz) **green
  cabbage**, finely shredded
salt and **pepper**

Meatballs
250 g (8 oz) **extra-lean
  minced beef**
40 g (1½ oz) **long-grain rice**
3 tablespoons chopped
  parsley, plus extra to garnish
¼ teaspoon **grated nutmeg**

Heat the butter in a large saucepan, add the onion and fry gently for 5 minutes until just turning golden around the edges. Stir in the diced root vegetables, the tomatoes and lemon.

Pour in the stock and lager, then add the spices and season well with salt and pepper. Bring to the boil, stirring, then cover and simmer for 45 minutes.

Meanwhile, mix all the meatball ingredients together. Divide into 18 and shape into small balls with wetted hands. Chill until needed.

Add the meatballs to the soup, bring the soup back to the boil then cover and simmer for 10 minutes. Add the cabbage and cook for 10 minutes until the cabbage is tender and the meatballs cooked all the way through. Taste and adjust the seasoning. Ladle into shallow bowls and sprinkle with a little chopped parsley if liked.

For beer broth with suet dumplings, gently fry 500 g (1 lb) thinly sliced onions in the butter for 20 minutes until very soft. Sprinkle with 2 teaspoons brown sugar and fry for 10 minutes, stirring until caramelized. Add the lemon slices, stock, lager and spices, omitting the root vegetables and tomatoes. Simmer for 20 minutes. Mix 100 g (3½ oz) self-raising flour with 50 g (2 oz) vegetable suet, 2 tablespoons chopped parsley and salt and pepper. Stir in 4 tablespoons water, then shape into small balls. Add to the simmering soup, cook for 10 minutes then ladle into bowls and serve.

cheesy butternut squash soup

Serves **6**

Preparation time **25 minutes**

Cooking time **about 1 hour**

2 tablespoons **olive oil**

1 **onion**, roughly chopped

1 **butternut squash**, about
750 g (1½ lb), halved,
deseeded, peeled and cut
into chunks

1–2 **garlic cloves**, finely
chopped

2 large fresh **sage sprigs**

1 litre (1¾ pints) **chicken** or
vegetable stock (see pages
10 and 13)

65 g (2½ oz) **Parmesan rinds**

salt and **pepper**

To finish

oil for deep frying

small bunch of **sage**

grated **Parmesan cheese**

Heat the oil in a saucepan, add the onion and fry for 5 minutes until softened and just beginning to turn golden. Add the squash, garlic and sage and fry for 5 minutes, stirring.

Pour in the stock and add the Parmesan rinds and salt and pepper. Bring to the boil then cover and simmer for 45 minutes until the squash is tender.

Scoop out and discard the sage and Parmesan rinds. Allow the soup to cool slightly, then purée in batches in a blender or food processor until smooth. Return to the saucepan and reheat. Add a little extra stock if needed then taste and adjust the seasoning.

Fill a small saucepan halfway with oil and heat until a cube of day-old bread sizzles the minute it is added. Then tear the sage leaves from the stems and add to the oil, frying for a minute or two until crisp. Lift out with a slotted spoon and put on to kitchen paper.

Ladle the soup into bowls, top with some of the crispy sage and a sprinkling of grated Parmesan, serving the remaining leaves and extra Parmesan in small bowls for diners to add their own as desired.

For Halloween pumpkin soup, fry the onion as above. Quarter a 1.5 kg (3 lb) pumpkin, scoop out the seeds, peel and cut into cubes and add to the onion and fry for 5 minutes. Stir in 1 teaspoon ground cumin, 1 teaspoon ground coriander and 1 teaspoon ground ginger instead of the garlic and sage, then pour in the stock. Cover and simmer for 30 minutes, then purée and reheat the soup as above. Serve with moon- and star-shaped croûtons cut with biscuit cutters.

beery oxtail & butter bean soup

Serves **6**
Preparation time **25 minutes**
Cooking time **4¼ hours**

1 tablespoon **sunflower oil**
500 g (1 lb) **oxtail pieces**,
  string removed
1 **onion**, finely chopped
2 **carrots**, diced
2 **celery sticks**, diced
200 g (7 oz) **potatoes**, diced
small bunch of **mixed herbs**
2 litres (3½ pints) **beef stock**
  (see page 12)
450 ml (¾ pint) **strong ale**
2 teaspoons **English mustard**
2 tablespoons **Worcestershire
  sauce**
1 tablespoon **tomato purée**
410 g (13½ oz) can **butter
  beans**, drained
salt and **pepper**
chopped **parsley**, to garnish

Heat the oil in a large saucepan, add the oxtail pieces and fry until browned on one side. Turn the oxtail pieces over and add the onion, stirring until browned on all sides. Stir in the carrots, celery, potatoes and herbs and cook for 2–3 more minutes.

Pour in the stock and ale, then add the mustard, Worcestershire sauce, tomato purée and butter beans. Season well with salt and pepper and bring to the boil, stirring. Half cover the pan and simmer gently for 4 hours.

Lift the oxtail and herbs out of the pan with a slotted spoon. Discard the herbs and cut the meat off the oxtail bones, discarding any fat. Return the meat to the pan, reheat then taste and adjust the seasoning if needed. Ladle into bowls, sprinkle with chopped parsley and serve with crusty bread.

For chillied oxtail & red bean soup, omit the bunch of mixed herbs and instead stir 2 finely chopped garlic cloves, 2 bay leaves, 1 teaspoon hot chilli powder, 1 teaspoon crushed cumin seeds and 1 teaspoon crushed coriander seeds into the vegetables. Then add the beef stock, a 400 g (13 oz) can chopped tomatoes, 1 tablespoon tomato purée and a drained 410 g (13½ oz) can of red kidney beans. Bring to the boil, simmer and finish as above.

kale soup with garlic croûtons

Serves **8–10**

Preparation time **20–25 minutes**

Cooking time **50 minutes**

50 g (2 oz) **butter** or **margarine**

1 **onion**, chopped

2 **carrots**, sliced

500 g (1 lb) **kale**, thick stems removed and discarded

1.2 litres (2 pints) **water**

600 ml (1 pint) **vegetable stock** (see page 13)

1 tablespoon **lemon juice**

300 g (10 oz) **potatoes**, peeled and sliced

pinch of **grated nutmeg**

salt and **pepper**

2 **kale leaves**, thinly shredded, to garnish

Garlic croûtons

6–8 slices of **white** or **brown bread**, crusts removed

6–8 tablespoons **olive oil**

3 **garlic cloves**, sliced

Melt the butter or margarine in a large saucepan, add the onion and fry for 5 minutes until softened and just beginning to turn golden. Add the carrots and kale in batches, stirring all the time, and cook for 2 minutes.

Add the water, stock, lemon juice, potatoes and nutmeg, with salt and pepper to taste. Bring to the boil, stirring from time to time. Lower the heat, cover and simmer for 35 minutes or until all the vegetables are soft. Purée the mixture in batches in a blender or food processor, adding extra water if it is too thick.

Prepare the croûtons by cutting the bread into 1 cm (½ inch) cubes. Heat the oil in a large frying pan, add the garlic and cook over a moderate heat for 1 minute. Add the bread squares and fry, turning frequently, until evenly golden brown. Transfer the croûtons to kitchen paper with a slotted spoon to drain. Discard the garlic, then add the thinly shredded kale to the pan and fry, stirring constantly until crispy.

Taste the soup and adjust the seasoning if needed and reheat without boiling. Serve in heated soup plates with the garlic croûtons and crispy kale.

For spiced kale soup, fry the onion as above, add the carrots and kale in batches then stir in 1 teaspoon smoked paprika and 2 chopped garlic cloves and cook for 2 minutes. Continue as above, adding ¼ teaspoon dried crushed red chilli to the oil when frying the croûtons.

something
special

cheat's bouillabaisse

Serves **6**
Preparation time **15 minutes**
Cooking time **30 minutes**

2 tablespoons **olive oil**
1 large **onion**, finely chopped
1 **leek**, thinly sliced
2 large pinches of **saffron threads**
2 **garlic cloves**, finely chopped
500 g (1 lb) **plum tomatoes**, skinned, roughly chopped
150 ml (¼ pint) **dry white wine**
600 ml (1 pint) **fish stock** (see page 13)
2–3 **thyme stems**, leaves torn from stems
500 g (1 lb) firm **white fish (monkfish, hake, haddock or cod)**, skinned and cubed
400 g (13 oz) **frozen mixed seafood**, defrosted, rinsed with cold water and drained
salt and **pepper**
½ small **French bread**, sliced and toasted

Heat the oil in a large saucepan, add the onion and leek and fry gently for 5 minutes, stirring until softened. Meanwhile soak the saffron in 1 tablespoon boiling water.

Add the garlic and tomatoes to the pan and fry for 2–3 minutes then mix in the soaked saffron, wine, stock, thyme and some salt and pepper. Cover and simmer for 10 minutes.

Add the white fish, re-cover and simmer gently for 3 minutes. Add the mixed seafood, re-cover and simmer gently for 5 more minutes until all the fish is just cooked. Ladle into bowls and serve with toasted bread topped with spoonfuls of rouille (see below).

For homemade rouille, to serve as an accompaniment, drain 3 roasted red peppers from a jar, put into a blender or food processor with 2–3 garlic cloves, 1 teaspoon finely chopped red chilli (from a jar), 1 slice white bread torn into pieces, a large pinch of saffron threads soaked in 1 tablespoon boiling water and 3 tablespoons olive oil. Blend until smooth and spoon into a small bowl.

pumpkin, orange & star anise soup

Serves **6**
Preparation time **25 minutes**
Cooking time **50 minutes**

25 g (1 oz) **butter**
1 **onion**, roughly chopped
1 small **pumpkin**, about 1.5 kg
   (3 lb), quartered, deseeded,
   peeled then diced
2 small **oranges**, rind removed
   with a zester, juice squeezed
1 litre (1¾ pints) **vegetable** or
   chicken stock (see pages
   13 and 10)
3 whole **star anise** or similar
   amount in pieces, plus extra
   to garnish
salt and **pepper**
crushed **black peppercorns**,
   to garnish (optional)

Heat the butter in a large saucepan, add the onion and fry gently for 5 minutes until softened. Add the pumpkin, toss in the butter and fry for 5 minutes, stirring.

Mix in the orange rind and juice, the stock and star anise. Season with salt and pepper and bring to the boil. Cover and simmer for 30 minutes, stirring occasionally until the pumpkin is soft. Scoop out the star anise and reserve.

Allow the soup to cool slightly, then purée in batches in a blender or food processor until smooth. Pour back into the saucepan and reheat. Taste and adjust the seasoning if needed.

Ladle the soup into bowls and garnish each bowl with a whole star anise and a sprinkling of black pepper, or a slice of spiced orange and chilli butter. Serve with sesame bread rolls.

For homemade spiced orange & chilli butter,

to serve as an accompaniment, beat 75 g (3 oz) butter with the grated rind of 1 orange, a large mild, deseeded and finely chopped red chilli, a pinch of ground turmeric and a pinch of ground cloves. Shape into a sausage then wrap in clingfilm. Chill then unwrap, slice and add to soup just before serving.

gingered cauliflower soup

Serves **6**
Preparation time **25 minutes**
Cooking time **25 minutes**

1 tablespoon **sunflower oil**
25 g (1 oz) **butter**
1 **onion**, roughly chopped
1 **cauliflower**, cut into florets,
   woody core discarded,
   about 500 g (1 lb) when
   prepared
3.5 cm (1½ inch) piece of
   fresh root ginger, peeled
   and finely chopped
900 ml (1½ pints) **vegetable**
   or **chicken stock** (see pages
   13 and 10)
300 ml (½ pint) **milk**
150 ml (¼ pint) **double**
   cream
salt and **pepper**

Soy-glazed seeds
1 tablespoon **sunflower oil**
2 tablespoons **sesame seeds**
2 tablespoons **sunflower**
   seeds
2 tablespoons **pumpkin**
   seeds
1 tablespoon **soy sauce**

Heat the oil and butter in a saucepan, add the onion and fry for 5 minutes until softened but not coloured. Stir in the cauliflower florets and ginger, then the stock. Season with salt and pepper and bring to the boil. Cover and simmer for 15 minutes until the cauliflower is just tender.

Meanwhile, make the glazed seeds by heating the oil in a frying pan, add the seeds and cook for 2–3 minutes, stirring until lightly browned. Add the soy sauce, then quickly cover the pan with a lid until the seeds have stopped popping. Set aside until ready to serve.

Purée the cooked soup in batches in a blender or food processor, then pour back into the saucepan and stir in the milk and half the cream. Bring just to the boil, then taste and adjust the seasoning if needed.

Ladle the soup into shallow bowls, drizzle over the rest of the cream and sprinkle with some of the glazed seeds, serving the remaining seeds in a small bowl for further sprinkling.

For creamy cauliflower & cashew soup, heat the oil and butter as above then add the chopped onion and 50 g (2 oz) cashew nuts and fry until the onions are softened and the nuts very lightly coloured. Mix in the cauliflower florets and stock as above, then season with salt, pepper and a little grated nutmeg. Simmer for 15 minutes. Purée and finish with milk and cream as above, ladle into bowls and garnish with 50 g (2 oz) cashew nuts fried in 15 g (½ oz) butter until pale golden, then cooked for 1–2 minutes more with 1 tablespoon honey until golden and caramelized.

spinach bouillabaisse

Serves **6**
Preparation time **15 minutes**
Cooking time **about 30
    minutes**

2 tablespoons **olive oil**
1 **onion**, finely chopped
1 **fennel bulb**, diced
400 g (13 oz) **potatoes**, diced
4 **garlic cloves**, finely
    chopped
3 large pinches of **saffron
    threads**
1.8 litres (3 pints) **vegetable**
    or **chicken stock** (see pages
    13 and 10)
150 ml (¼ pint) **dry white
    wine**
125 g (4 oz) **baby leaf
    spinach**, rinsed and drained
6 **eggs**
salt and **pepper**

Heat the oil in a large saucepan (or shallow sauté pan if possible) then add the onion and fry for 5 minutes until just beginning to soften. Add the fennel, reserving any green fronds for later, the potato and the garlic and fry for 5 more minutes, stirring.

Mix in the saffron, stock and white wine, then season with salt and pepper and bring to the boil. Cover and simmer for 15 minutes, stirring occasionally or until the potatoes are tender.

Add the spinach, tearing the larger leaves into pieces and cook for 2–3 minutes until just beginning to wilt. Taste and adjust the seasoning if needed. Scoop out most of the vegetables with a slotted spoon and divide between warmed shallow serving bowls. Add the eggs one at a time to the remaining hot stock, leaving a little space between them and simmer gently for 3–4 minutes until the whites are just set and the yolks are cooked to your liking.

Lift the poached eggs out of the soup carefully with a slotted spoon and place on top of the vegetables in the soup bowls. Ladle the stock around the eggs, top with any reserved and snipped green fennel fronds and sprinkle with black pepper. Serve with toasted olive ciabatta bread.

For creamy spinach & fennel soup, make the soup as above, with 1.2 litres (2 pints) stock and 150 ml (¼ pint) white wine. Purée the soup in batches in a blender or food processor when the spinach has just wilted. Reheat, omit the eggs, and serve topped with spoonfuls of crème fraîche and some fennel or dill fronds.

apple & celery soup

Serves **6**

Preparation time **25 minutes**

Cooking time **about 40 minutes**

25 g (1 oz) **butter**

1 **onion**, roughly chopped

1 **baking potato**, about 250 g (8 oz), diced

1 **cooking apple**, about 250 g (8 oz), quartered, cored, peeled then diced

1 **head of celery**, base trimmed

750 ml (1¼ pints) **chicken** or **vegetable stock** (see pages 10 and 13)

300 ml (½ pint) **milk**

salt and **pepper**

Stilton & walnut cream

50 g (2 oz) **Stilton**, rind removed, cheese diced

25 g (1 oz) **walnut pieces**, chopped

6 tablespoons **full-fat crème fraîche**

2 tablespoons chopped **chives** or tops of 2 **spring onions**, chopped

Heat the butter in a saucepan, add the onion and fry for 5 minutes until just beginning to soften. Stir in the potato and apple, cover and fry gently for 10 minutes, stirring occasionally.

Reserve the tiny celery leaves from the centre of the celery for garnish and keep in a bowl of cold water until needed. Thickly slice the rest of the stems and add with the larger leaves to the onion and stir-fry for 2–3 minutes. Pour on the stock then season with salt and pepper and bring to the boil. Cover and simmer for 15 minutes until the celery is soft but still a pale green.

Purée the soup in batches in a blender or food processor until smooth. Return to the saucepan, stir in the milk and then reheat. Taste and adjust the seasoning if needed.

Stir half the diced cheese and half the walnuts into the crème fraîche, then mix in the chives or spring onion and a little salt and pepper. Ladle the soup into shallow bowls, then spoon the crème fraîche mixture into the centre. Sprinkle with the remaining cheese and nuts and add a little black pepper.

For apple & parsnip soup, omit the potato and celery adding 625 g (1¼ lb) diced parsnips when frying the apple. Stir in 1½ teaspoons crushed cumin seeds and ½ teaspoon turmeric, then mix in 900 ml (1½ pints) of vegetable or chicken stock and season. Bring to the boil then cover and simmer for 45 minutes. Purée and reheat with the milk. Make the Stilton and crème fraîche mixture as above, adding ½ teaspoon finely chopped red chilli instead of the walnuts.

oriental mussel soup

Serves **4**

Preparation time **25 minutes**

Cooking time **20–25 minutes**

1 tablespoon **sunflower oil**

3 **spring onions**, sliced

½ **red pepper**, cored, deseeded, diced

1 **garlic clove**, finely chopped

2.5 cm (1 inch) piece of **fresh root ginger**, peeled and grated

3 teaspoons **ready-made red Thai curry paste**

400 ml (14 fl oz) can **full-fat coconut milk**

450 ml (¾ pint) **fish** or **vegetable stock** (see page 13)

2 teaspoons **Thai fish sauce**

grated rind of **1 lime**

small bunch of **coriander**

500 g (1 lb) **mussels**, scrubbed and beards removed, any cracked or open mussels discarded

Heat the oil in a large shallow saucepan, add the spring onions, red pepper, garlic and ginger and fry for 2 minutes. Stir in the curry paste and cook for 1 minute, then mix in the coconut milk, stock, fish sauce and lime rind. Bring to the boil and simmer for 5 minutes.

Snip half the coriander into the soup using scissors. Add the mussels then cover and cook for 8–10 minutes until the mussels have opened.

Scoop the mussels out of the soup with a slotted spoon and put on to a large plate. Discard any shut mussels then reserve half the opened mussels in their shells for garnish. Take the remaining mussels out of their shells and stir them back into the soup. Ladle the soup into bowls, top with the reserved mussels in shells and garnish with the remaining snipped coriander. Serve with warm crusty bread for dunking into the soup.

For saffron mussel soup, fry 3 sliced spring onions, 2 cloves finely chopped garlic, ½–1 deseeded and finely chopped large mild red chilli according to taste, ½ a red pepper and ½ a yellow or orange pepper, deseeded and diced in 1 tablespoon olive oil until softened. Add 3 large pinches of saffron threads, 150 ml (¼ pint) white wine and 750 ml (1¼ pints) fish or vegetable stock. Season with salt and pepper and simmer for 5 minutes. Add the mussels as above then cover and simmer until the shells have opened. Serve in shallow bowls garnished with snipped parsley.

crab bisque

Serves **6**
Preparation time **20 minutes**
Cooking time **25 minutes**

25 g (1 oz) **butter**
1 **onion**, roughly chopped
2 tablespoons **brandy**
40 g (1½ oz) **long-grain rice**
300 ml (½ pint) **fish stock**
(see page 13)
150 g (5 oz) **prepared crab
on the shell**, plus **1 extra
crab**, to garnish (optional)
2 canned **anchovy fillets**,
drained and chopped
½ teaspoon **mild paprika**
200 ml (7 fl oz) **milk**
150 ml (¼ pint) **double
cream**
salt and **cayenne pepper**

Heat the butter in a saucepan, add the onion and fry gently for 5 minutes until softened. Add the brandy and when boiling, flame with a long match and quickly stand back. As soon as the flames have subsided stir in the rice and add the stock.

Scoop the dark and white crab meat out of the shell into the pan and then mix in the chopped anchovies and paprika. Season with a little salt and cayene pepper then bring to the boil. Cover and simmer for 20 minutes.

Allow the soup to cool slightly then purée in batches in a blender or food processor. Pour back into the saucepan and stir in the milk and cream. Reheat, but take care to bring just to the boil and then reduce the heat to a simmer, stirring until hot all the way through. Taste and adjust the seasoning if needed.

Pour into teacups. Pick out the crab meat from the extra crab (if using) and flake into pieces. Serve in a separate bowl for diners to sprinkle over their soup and garnish with a little extra paprika.

For crab & salmon chowder, fry the onion in butter as above. Add 200 g (7 oz) diced potato and fry for 5 minutes. Add 2 tablespoons brandy and flame as above. Mix in 600 ml (1 pint) fish stock, the dark and white crab meat, anchovies and paprika as above. Cover and simmer for 15 minutes. Add 300 g (10 oz) salmon fillet, cut into 2 thick slices, cover and simmer for 10 minutes. Lift out the salmon, peel off the skin, break into flakes and discard any bones. Return the salmon to the soup, stir in 200 ml (7 fl oz) milk and 150 ml (¼ pint) double cream. Reheat and serve.

spinach soup with haddock

Serves **6**

Preparation time **30 minutes**

Cooking time **about 1 hour**

25 g (1 oz) **butter**

1 **onion**, roughly chopped

1 **baking potato**, about 250 g (8 oz), diced

1 litre (1¾ pints) **vegetable** or **chicken stock** (see pages 13 and 10)

¼ teaspoon **grated nutmeg**

225 g (7½ oz) **young spinach leaves**, rinsed and drained

300 ml (½ pint) **milk**

400 g (13 oz) **smoked haddock**

9 **quail's eggs**

2 **egg yolks**

150 ml (¼ pint) **double cream**

salt and **pepper**

Heat the butter in a saucepan, add the onion and fry gently for 5 minutes until softened. Add the potato, cover and cook for 10 minutes, stirring occasionally.

Pour in the stock, add the nutmeg and salt and pepper then bring to the boil. Cover and simmer for 20 minutes until the potato is soft. Reserve a few tiny spinach leaves and add the rest to the pan. Re-cover the pan and cook for 5 minutes until just wilted.

Purée the soup in batches in a blender or food processor until smooth, then pour back into the saucepan, mix in the milk and set aside.

Cut the haddock into two pieces, cook in a steamer for 8–10 minutes until the fish flakes when pressed with a knife. Put the quail's eggs into a small saucepan of cold water, bring to the boil and simmer for 2–3 minutes, drain, rinse with cold water and peel off shells.

Mix the 2 hen egg yolks with the double cream. Stir into the soup and bring just to the boil, still stirring. Taste and adjust the seasoning if needed. Flake the fish, discarding the skin and bones, make small mounds in the base of 6 shallow serving bowls and top with the quail's egg halves. Ladle the soup around the fish and eggs and garnish with tiny spinach leaves and pepper.

For cream of nettle soup, make up the soup as above using 200 g (7 oz) young nettle tops instead of the spinach. (Pick nettles using rubber gloves so that you don't get stung and rinse the leaves well in cold water.) Purée the soup in a blender or food processor and finish with milk, egg yolks and cream, as above. Garnish with diced smoked ham.

smooth carrot soup with mint oil

Serves **6**
Preparation time **20 minutes**
Cooking time **1–1¼ hours**

2 tablespoons **olive oil**
1 **onion**, roughly chopped
750 g (1½ lb) **carrots**, diced
40 g (1½ oz) **long-grain rice**
1 litre (1¾ pints) **vegetable** or
 chicken stock (see pages
 13 and 10)
300 ml (½ pint) **milk**

Mint oil
15 g (½ oz) **fresh mint**
¼ teaspoon **caster sugar**
3 tablespoons **olive oil**
salt and **pepper**

Heat the oil in a saucepan, add the onion and fry for 5 minutes until just beginning to soften and turn golden around the edges. Stir in the carrots and cook for 5 minutes. Mix in the rice, stock and a little salt and pepper. Bring to the boil then cover and simmer for 45 minutes, stirring occasionally until the carrots are tender.

Meanwhile make the mint oil. Strip the leaves from the mint stems and add the leaves to a blender or food processor with the sugar and a little pepper. Finely chop then gradually blend in the oil a little at a time with the motor running. Spoon into a small bowl and stir before using.

Rinse the blender or food processor, then purée the soup in batches until smooth. Return the soup to the saucepan and stir in the milk. Reheat then taste and adjust the seasoning if needed. Ladle into bowls then drizzle with the mint oil and add some extra mint leaves if liked. Serve with muffins.

For courgette muffins, to serve as an accompaniment, put 300 g (10 oz) self-raising flour into a bowl, and add 3 teaspoons baking powder, 75 g (3 oz) freshly grated Parmesan cheese, 200 g (7 oz) coarsely grated courgette, 150 ml (5 oz) low-fat natural yogurt, 3 tablespoons olive oil, 3 eggs and 3 tablespoons milk. Fork together until just mixed, and divide into a 12-hole muffin tin lined with paper cases. Bake in a preheated oven, 200°C (400°F), Gas Mark 6, for 18–20 minutes until well risen and golden brown. Serve warm.

clam, potato & bean soup

Serves **6**
Preparation time **30 minutes**
Cooking time **45 minutes**

2 tablespoons **olive oil**
125 g (4 oz) piece of
   unsmoked pancetta, diced
1 **onion**, chopped
375 g (12 oz) **potatoes**, diced
1 **leek**, sliced
2 **garlic cloves**, crushed
1 tablespoon chopped
   rosemary
2 **bay leaves**
400 g (13 oz) can **cannellini**
   beans, drained
900 ml (1½ pints) **vegetable**
   stock (see page 13)
1 kg (2 lb) small **clams** or
   mussels, scrubbed
salt and **pepper**

Garlic & parsley oil
150 ml (¼ pint) **extra virgin**
   olive oil
2 large **garlic cloves**, sliced
¼ teaspoon **salt**
1 tablespoon chopped
   parsley

Heat the oil in a large saucepan and fry the pancetta for 5 minutes until golden. Remove from the pan with a slotted spoon and set aside. Add the onion, potatoes, leek, garlic, rosemary and bay leaves to the pan and fry gently for 10 minutes until softened. Add the beans and stock, bring to the boil and simmer gently for 20 minutes, until the vegetables are tender.

Meanwhile, make the garlic and parsley oil. Heat the oil with the garlic and salt in a small pan and simmer gently for 3 minutes. Leave to cool, then stir in the parsley. Set aside.

Transfer half of the soup to a blender or food processor and purée until really smooth, then pour it back into the pan and season with salt and pepper. Stir in the clams or mussels and return the pancetta to the soup. Simmer gently until the shellfish are open, about 5 minutes (discard any that remain closed). Spoon the soup into bowls and drizzle with the garlic and parsley oil and serve with some crusty bread.

For clam, tomato & bean soup, fry 125 g (4 oz) diced chorizo in the oil instead of the pancetta, then drain and reserve. Fry the onion, potato, leek, garlic and herbs, then add 4 large diced tomatoes (skinning them first if preferred), the beans and stock. Simmer for 20 minutes. Purée half the soup then add the shellfish and fried chorizo and cook and serve as above with the garlic and parsley oil.

chicken & tarragon with puff pastry

Serves **6**
Preparation time **40 minutes**
Cooking time **about 1¾ hours**

6 **chicken thighs**
1 **carrot**, sliced
2 **celery sticks**, sliced
200 g (7 oz) **leeks**, sliced
  thinly, white and green parts
  kept separate
900 ml (1½ pints) **chicken
  stock** (see page 10)
200 ml (7 fl oz) **white wine**
50 g (2 oz) **butter**
25 g (1 oz) **plain flour**
grated rind ½ **orange**
2 teaspoons **Dijon mustard**
1 tablespoon chopped
  tarragon
425 g (14 oz) **frozen pack
  ready-rolled puff pastry
  sheets**, defrosted
1 **egg**, beaten to glaze
salt and **pepper**

Put the chicken thighs into a large saucepan with the carrot, celery and white sliced leeks. Pour on the stock, wine, salt and pepper. Bring to the boil, then cover and simmer gently for 1 hour until the chicken is very tender.

Strain the chicken stock into a measuring jug, drain the chicken and vegetables then transfer the chicken to a chopping board and cut the meat into small pieces discarding the skin and bones and vegetables. If the stock measures more than 900 ml (1½ pints) return it to the saucepan and boil rapidly until reduced.

Melt the butter in a smaller saucepan, add the green sliced leeks and fry for 2–3 minutes until softened. Stir in the flour and cook briefly, then gradually mix in the strained stock and bring to the boil, stirring until the sauce has thickened slightly. Stir in the orange rind, mustard and tarragon. Taste and adjust the seasoning if needed. Divide the diced chicken between 6 x 300 ml (½ pint) ovenproof dishes so that the soup three-quarter fills the dishes (any more and they will overflow during baking).

Unroll the pastry, cut 6 circles slightly larger than the tops of the dishes, then 6 long strips about 1 cm (½ inch) wide from the trimmings. Brush the dish rims with a little egg, stick the pastry strips around the rims, then brush these with egg before sticking the pastry lids in place. Flute the edges of the pastry with a small knife then slash the lids lightly. Brush with egg, sprinkle with a little salt and bake in a preheated oven, 200°C (400°F), Gas Mark 6, for 20–25 minutes until golden and the soup is bubbling underneath. Stand the dishes on small plates and serve immediately.

venison, red wine & lentil soup

Serves **6**
Preparation time **20 minutes**
Cooking time **about 1½ hours**

6 **venison sausages**
1 tablespoon **olive oil**
1 **onion**, roughly chopped
2 **garlic cloves**, finely
   chopped
200 g (7 oz) **potatoes**, diced
1 **carrot**, diced
4 **tomatoes**, skinned if liked,
   roughly chopped
125 g (4 oz) **green lentils**
300 ml (½ pint) **red wine**
1.5 litres (2½ pints) **beef** or
   pheasant stock (see pages
   12 and 11)
2 tablespoons **cranberry
   sauce**
1 tablespoon **tomato purée**
1 teaspoon **ground allspice**
thyme sprig
2 **bay leaves**
salt and **pepper**

Grill the sausages until browned and just cooked. Meanwhile heat the oil in a large saucepan, add the onion and fry for 5 minutes until softened and just beginning to brown. Add the garlic, potato and carrot and fry briefly, then mix in the tomatoes and lentils.

Pour in the wine and stock, then add the cranberry sauce, tomato purée, allspice and herbs. Season well with salt and pepper then slice the sausages and add these to the pan. Bring to the boil, stirring, then cover and simmer gently for 1¼ hours. Taste and adjust seasoning if needed.

Ladle the soup into bowls and serve with French bread croûtons (see page 15) rubbed with a little garlic and sprinkled with parsley.

For pheasant, bacon & black pudding soup, omit the sausages, adding instead 150 g (5 oz) diced smoked streaky bacon when frying the onion. Add 125 (4 oz) diced black pudding and the leftover diced meat from a roast pheasant along with the potato, carrot, tomatoes and lentils. Continue as above, adding pheasant stock in place of beef stock.

mushroom & madeira soup

Serves **6**
Preparation time **30 minutes**
Cooking time **40 minutes**

50 g (2 oz) **butter**
1 tablespoon **olive oil**
1 **onion**, chopped
400 g (13 oz) **cup mushrooms**, sliced
2 large **flat mushrooms**, sliced
2 **garlic cloves**, finely chopped
125 ml (4 fl oz) **Madeira** or **medium sherry**
900 ml (1½ pints) **chicken** or **vegetable stock** (see pages 10 and 13)
40 g (1½ oz) **long-grain rice**
2 **thyme sprigs**
450 ml (¾ pint) **milk**
150 ml (¼ pint) **double cream**
salt and **pepper**

To garnish
25 g (1 oz) **butter**
250 g (8 oz) pack **exotic mushrooms**
few extra **thyme leaves**

Heat the butter and oil in a large saucepan, add the onion and fry gently for 5 minutes until just turning golden around the edges. Add the mushrooms and garlic and fry over a high heat for 2–3 minutes until golden.

Stir in the Madeira, stock, rice and thyme, then season with salt and pepper and bring to the boil. Cover and simmer for 30 minutes.

Allow the soup to cool slightly and discard the thyme sprigs. Purée the soup in batches in a blender or food processor until smooth. Return to the saucepan and stir in the milk and cream. Reheat without boiling, then taste and adjust the seasoning if needed.

Make the garnish by heating the remaining butter in a frying pan and slicing any large exotic mushrooms, then add them to the pan and fry for 2 minutes until golden. Ladle the soup into shallow soup bowls and gently spoon the mushrooms into the centre. Garnish with a few thyme leaves and serve with scones (see below).

For baby walnut scones, to serve as an accompaniment, rub 50 g (2 oz) butter into 250 g (8 oz) self-raising flour. Season and mix in 50 g (2 oz) roughly chopped walnuts, 2 teaspoons thyme leaves and 75 g (3 oz) grated mature Cheddar cheese. Mix in ½ a beaten egg and 8–10 tablespoons milk to make a soft dough. Knead lightly, then roll out to 2.5 cm (1 inch) thickness. Stamp out 5 cm (2 inch) circles. Put on a greased baking sheet, brush with remaining ½ egg, then bake in a preheated oven, 200°C (400°F), Gas Mark 6, for 10–12 minutes. Serve warm.

chestnut soup with truffle oil

Serves **6**
Preparation time **30 minutes**
Cooking time **1¼ hours**

500 g (1 lb) **fresh chestnuts**
50 g (2 oz) **butter**
1 **onion**, finely chopped
10 **smoked streaky bacon
rashers**
200 g (7 oz) **potatoes**, diced
4 tablespoons **brandy**, plus a
little extra to serve
900 ml (1½ pints) **pheasant**
or **beef stock** (see pages
11 and 12)
fresh thyme sprig
large pinch of **ground
cinnamon**
large pinch of **grated nutmeg**
salt and **pepper**
little **truffle oil**, to garnish
(optional)

Make a cross cut in the top of each chestnut then
add to a saucepan of boiling water and poach for
15 minutes. Drain into a colander, rinse with cold water
so that they are cool enough to handle, then remove
the skins with a small sharp knife and roughly chop.

Heat the butter in a saucepan, add the onion and fry
gently for 5 minutes until just beginning to turn golden
around the edges. Dice 4 rashers of the bacon and add
to the pan along with the potato and chestnuts. Fry
gently for 5 minutes, stirring occasionally.

Add the brandy and, when bubbling, flame with a long
taper and quickly stand back. As soon as the flames
have subsided pour in the stock. Add the thyme, spices
and seasoning and bring to the boil, cover and simmer
for 45 minutes.

Discard the thyme sprig and purée half the soup in a
blender or food processor until smooth. Return to the
soup in the pan and reheat. Taste and adjust the
seasoning if needed. Wrap each remaining rasher of
bacon around a skewer and grill until crisp. Ladle the
soup into cups and top with the bacon skewers. Drizzle
with the truffle oil and a little extra brandy if liked.

For walnut & celeriac soup, fry the onion in butter as
above. Add 4 diced smoked streaky bacon rashers,
375 g (12 oz) peeled and diced celeriac instead of
the potato and 200 g (7 oz) walnut pieces. Fry gently
for 5 minutes. Omit the brandy, stir in the stock, thyme
and spices and simmer for 45 minutes. Purée and add
a little extra stock if needed. Reheat and serve with
croûtons (see page 15).

sweetcorn & celery soup

Serves **6**
Preparation time **25 minutes**
Cooking time **30 minutes**

50 g (2 oz) **butter**
1 **onion**, chopped
4 **corn on the cob**, green
   leaves removed, kernels cut
   from cobs
3 **celery sticks**, sliced
2 **garlic cloves**, finely
   chopped
1 litre (1¾ pints) **chicken** or
   vegetable stock (see pages
   10 and 13)
2 **bay leaves**
salt and **cayenne pepper**

Heat the butter in a saucepan, add the onion and fry gently for 5 minutes until just beginning to turn golden around the edges. Add the corn, celery and garlic and fry for 5 minutes.

Pour in the stock, add the bay leaves, salt and pepper and bring to the boil. Cover and simmer for 20 minutes.

Discard the bay leaves then allow the soup to cool slightly. Purée the soup in batches in a blender or food processor until smooth. Return to the saucepan and reheat. Taste and adjust the seasoning if needed. Ladle into bowls and top with spoonfuls of chilli and tomato chutney (see below).

For chilli & tomato chutney, to serve as an accompaniment, heat 1 tablespoon sunflower oil in a small saucepan, add ½ a finely chopped red onion, 1 cored, deseeded and diced red pepper and 1–2 large mild, cored, deseeded and finely chopped red chillies, to taste. Fry gently for 5 minutes until softened, then mix in 4 chopped tomatoes (skinned if liked), 4 tablespoons caster sugar, 2 tablespoons red wine vinegar and a little salt and pepper. Simmer for 15 minutes, stirring occasionally until thick.

lentil, pancetta & scallop soup

Serves **4**
Preparation time **15 minutes**
Cooking time **about 40 minutes**

50 g (2 oz) **puy lentils**
1 tablespoon **olive oil**
1 small **leek**, diced
75 g (3 oz) diced **pancetta**
1 **garlic clove**, finely chopped
4 tablespoons **Pernod**
600 ml (1 pint) **fish stock** (see page 13)
grated rind of ½ **lemon**
150 ml (¼ pint) **double cream**
small bunch of **parsley**
25 g (1 oz) **butter**
200 g (7 oz) bag **frozen baby scallops**, defrosted
salt and **pepper**

Bring a saucepan of water to the boil, add the lentils and simmer for 20 minutes until just tender. Drain into a sieve, rinse and drain again and set aside. Wash and dry the pan.

Heat the oil in the cleaned pan then add the leek, pancetta and garlic and fry for 5 minutes, stirring until the pancetta is just beginning to turn golden. Add the Pernod and, when bubbling, flame with a long taper and quickly stand well back. As soon as the flames subside pour in the stock. Add the lemon rind and a little salt and pepper, then bring to the boil and simmer uncovered for 10 minutes.

Stir in the cooked lentils, cream and parsley, then taste and adjust the seasoning if needed. Heat the butter in a frying pan. Rinse the scallops in cold water and drain well, then add to the pan and fry for 3–4 minutes, turning until golden and cooked through.

Ladle the soup into shallow bowls and spoon the scallops into a small mound in the centre.

For creamy pancetta & mussel soup, make up the soup as above. When the stock has cooked for 10 minutes, add 500 g (1 lb) closed mussels that have been scrubbed and had their beards removed. Cover and simmer for 8–10 minutes until the mussels have opened. Discard any that are still closed then spoon into bowls. Stir the cream and parsley into the soup, then ladle over the mussels.

five-spice duck soup & pak choi

Serves **4**

Preparation time **15 minutes**

Cooking time **20 minutes**

1.2 litres (2 pints) **duck stock** (see page 11)

grated rind and juice of **1 orange**

4 tablespoons **medium sherry**

¼ teaspoon **five spice powder**

5 cm (2 inch) piece of **fresh root ginger**, thinly sliced

1 tablespoon **soy sauce**

2 tablespoons **Chinese plum sauce**

125–175 g (4–6 oz) **leftover cooked duck**, stripped from carcass before stock was made

½ bunch of **spring onions**, thinly sliced

2 **pak choi**, thickly sliced

salt and **pepper** (optional)

Pour the stock into a saucepan then add the orange rind and juice, sherry, spice powder and ginger. Stir in the soy sauce and plum sauce then bring to the boil, stirring. Cover and simmer gently for 15 minutes.

Add the duck, spring onions and pak choi and simmer for 5 minutes. Taste and add a little salt and pepper if needed then ladle into bowls.

For herbed duck broth with noodles, soak 50 g (2 oz) fine dried egg noodles in boiling water for 5 minutes. Heat 1.2 litres (2 pints) duck stock as above and substitute the orange rind and juice with that of ½ a lemon. Omit the sherry and spice powder, but add the ginger and soy sauce, cover and simmer as above. Add 3 tablespoons fresh chopped parsley and 3 tablespoons fresh chopped mint, then add the leftover cooked shredded duck, salt and pepper and simmer for 5 minutes. Divide the noodles between the bowls and ladle the broth over the top.

salmon & tarragon sabayon

Serves **6**
Preparation time **10 minutes**
Cooking time **15 minutes**

400 g (13 oz) **salmon**, cut
   into two
4 tablespoons **Noilly Prat**
4 **spring onions**, thinly sliced,
   white and green parts kept
   separate
pared rind of **1 lemon**
600 ml (1 pint) **fish stock**
   (see page 13)
4 **egg yolks**
1 tablespoon finely chopped
   fresh **tarragon**
1 teaspoon **Dijon mustard**
25 g (1 oz) **butter**, at room
   temperature
150 ml (¼ pint) **double**
   cream
salt and **pepper**
tarragon sprigs, to garnish
   (optional)

Put the salmon pieces into a saucepan with the Noilly Prat, white sliced spring onions, lemon rind and the stock. Season with salt and pepper and bring to the boil. Cover and simmer for 10 minutes until the fish is cooked and flakes easily when pressed with a knife.

Lift the fish out of the stock and break into pieces, carefully checking for any bones. Keep hot under foil.

Whisk the egg yolks, tarragon, mustard and butter together in a large bowl. Strain the stock, then gradually whisk it into the egg mixture until smooth. Pour into the saucepan, add the cream and green sliced spring onions, then whisk over a low heat for 4–5 minutes until the mixture is frothy and slightly thickened. Take care not to overheat the soup or the eggs will curdle. Taste and adjust the seasoning if needed.

Divide the salmon between 6 shallow serving bowls, pour the hot frothy sabayon around the salmon and garnish with tarragon, if liked. Serve with melba toast.

For melba toast, to serve as an accompaniment, lightly toast 4 slices of bread on both sides. Trim off the crusts then cut in half horizontally through the bread to make 8 very thin slices. Cut the slices into triangles then put on to a baking sheet, untoasted side upwards and grill until the corners of the bread begin to curl.

vegetable broth with wontons

Serves **6**

Preparation time **40 minutes**, plus marinading

Cooking time **5 minutes**

Wontons

125 g (4 oz) **pork mince**

½ teaspoon **cornflour**

1 teaspoon **sesame oil**

2 tablespoons **soy sauce**

1 small **garlic clove**, finely chopped

43 g (1¾ oz) can **dark crab meat**

1 **egg**, separated

18 x 9 cm (3¾ inch) square **wonton wrappers**

Broth

1.2 litres (2 pints) **chicken stock** (see page 10)

1 bunch **asparagus**, trimmed, thickly sliced

75 g (3 oz) **mangetout**, sliced

4 **spring onions**, thinly sliced

4 teaspoons **fish sauce**

4 tablespoons **dry sherry**

small bunch of **coriander**, two thirds roughly chopped, the remaining sprigs to garnish

Mix all the wonton ingredients together except the egg white and wrappers and chill for 30 minutes for the flavours to marinade. Separate the wonton wrappers, add a heaped teaspoonful of the pork mixture on to each, brush the edges of the wrapper with a little egg white, then bring the edges up and over the filling and twist together to make mini parcels.

Put all the broth ingredients into a large saucepan, bring to the boil then add the wontons and simmer for 5 minutes until the filling is cooked through. Ladle into bowls and garnish with coriander sprigs.

For vegetable broth with chillied tuna, make up the broth as above but omit the wontons. Rub a 200 g (7 oz) thick cut tuna steak with 1 teaspoon sesame oil and 1 teaspoon sunflower oil, 1 deseeded and finely chopped red chilli and 1 clove finely chopped garlic. Add to a preheated frying pan and fry for 1½ minutes each side until the top and bottom are browned and the centre still pink. Thinly slice and divide between soup bowls. Ladle the broth around the tuna and serve immediately otherwise the soup will overcook the tuna.

chorizo, fennel & potato soup

Serves **8–10**
Preparation time **15 minutes**
Cooking time **30 minutes**

3 tablespoons **olive oil**
1 **onion**, chopped
400 g (13 oz) **fennel bulb**,
  chopped
150 g (5 oz) **chorizo**, cut into
  small pieces
500 g (1 lb) floury **potatoes**,
  cut into small dice
1 litre (1¾ pints) **chicken** or
  ham stock (see page 10)
3 tablespoons finely chopped
  coriander
3 tablespoons **crème fraîche**
salt and **pepper**

Heat the oil in a large saucepan and gently fry the onion and fennel for about 10 minutes until they are very soft and beginning to brown.

Add the chorizo, potatoes and stock and bring to the boil. Reduce the heat, cover with a lid and cook gently for 20 minutes until the potatoes are very tender.

Blend the soup until fairly smooth in a blender or food processor. Stir in the coriander and crème fraîche and heat through gently for a couple of minutes. Season with salt and pepper to taste and serve in small, warmed cups.

For chorizo, celery & potato soup, fry the onion in the oil as above, adding 400 g (13 oz) chopped celery instead of the fennel. Continue as the recipe but serve without puréeing, stirring the coriander and crème fraîche through just before serving.

healthy
soups

pesto & lemon soup

Serves **6**
Preparation time **10 minutes**
Cooking time **25 minutes**

1 tablespoon **olive oil**
1 **onion**, finely chopped
2 **garlic cloves**, finely
    chopped
2 **tomatoes**, skinned,
    chopped
1.2 litres (2 pints) **vegetable
    stock** (see page 13)
3 teaspoons **pesto**, plus extra
    to serve
grated rind and juice of
    1 **lemon**
100 g (3½ oz) **broccoli**, cut
    into small florets, stems
    sliced
150 g (5 oz) **courgettes**,
    diced
100 g (3½ oz) **frozen green
    soya beans**
65 g (2½ oz) small **pasta
    shapes**
50 g (2 oz) **spinach**, shredded
salt and **pepper**
fresh **basil leaves**, to garnish
    (optional)

Heat the oil in a saucepan, add the onion and fry gently for 5 minutes, stirring occasionally until softened. Add the garlic, tomatoes, stock, pesto, lemon rind and a little salt and pepper and simmer gently for 10 minutes.

Add the broccoli, courgettes, soya beans and pasta shapes, then simmer for 6 minutes. Add the spinach and lemon juice and cook for 2 minutes until the spinach has just wilted and the pasta is cooked.

Ladle into bowls, top with extra spoonfuls of pesto and garnish with a sprinkling of basil leaves. Serve with warm olive or sun-dried tomato focaccia or ciabatta bread or Parmesan thins.

For homemade Parmesan thins, to serve as an accompaniment, line a baking sheet with non-stick baking paper then sprinkle 100 g (3½ oz) freshly grated Parmesan cheese into 18 well-spaced mounds. Cook in a preheated oven, 190°C (375°F), Gas Mark 5, for about 5 minutes, or until the cheese has melted and is just beginning to brown. Leave to cool and harden, then peel off the paper and serve on the side with the soup.

seafood gumbo

Serves **6**
Preparation time **20 minutes**
Cooking time **30 minutes**

1 tablespoon **sunflower oil**
1 **onion**, finely chopped
1 small **carrot**, diced
1 **celery stick**, diced
½ **red pepper**, cored,
  deseeded and diced
425 g (14 oz) **tomatoes**,
  skinned if liked, roughly
  chopped
large **thyme sprig**
¼ teaspoon crushed **chilli
  flakes**
2 teaspoons **tomato purée**
1 litre (1¾ pints) **vegetable** or
  fish stock (see page 13)
40 g (1½ oz) **long-grain rice**
400 g (13 oz) pack **frozen
  seafood selection**,
  defrosted, rinsed with cold
  water and drained
43 g (1½ oz) can
  dressed crab
75 g (3 oz) **okra**, trimmed,
  sliced
salt and **pepper**
few extra **thyme leaves**, to
  garnish (optional)

Heat the oil in a saucepan, add the onion and fry gently for 5 minutes until softened and just beginning to brown. Stir in the carrot, celery and red pepper and fry for a few more minutes. Mix in the tomatoes, thyme, chilli and tomato purée, then pour in the stock. Add the rice, season with salt and pepper and bring to the boil.

Cover and simmer for 20 minutes, stirring occasionally. Halve any very large mussels, then stir into the soup with the remaining seafood, canned crab and okra. Cover and simmer for 5 minutes, then taste and adjust the seasoning if needed. Ladle into bowls and sprinkle with a few thyme leaves, if liked. Serve with crusty bread.

For chicken & ham gumbo, fry 6 diced, skinned and boned chicken thighs along with the onion. Continue making the soup as above, adding in 50 g (2 oz) diced ham and 75 g (3 oz) sliced green beans instead of the seafood, crab and okra. Finish and serve as above.

summer vegetable soup

Serves **4**
Preparation time **15 minutes**
Cooking time **about 25 minutes**

1 teaspoon **olive oil**
1 **leek**, finely sliced
1 large **potato**, peeled and chopped
450 g (14½ oz) **mixed summer vegetables** (such as peas, asparagus, broad beans and courgettes)
2 tablespoons chopped **mint**
900 ml (1½ pints) **vegetable stock** (see page 13)
2 tablespoons **low-fat crème fraîche**
salt and **pepper**

Heat the oil in a medium saucepan and fry the leek for 3–4 minutes until softened.

Add the potato and stock to the pan and cook for 10 minutes. Add all the remaining vegetables and the mint, then bring to the boil. Reduce the heat and simmer for 10 minutes.

Transfer the soup to a blender or food processor and purée until smooth. Return the soup to the pan, add the crème fraîche and season to taste with salt and pepper. Heat through gently and serve.

For chunky summer vegetable soup with mixed herb gremolata, make up the soup as above but do not purée. Ladle the soup into bowls and serve topped with 2 tablespoons of crème fraîche and gremolata made by mixing 2 tablespoons chopped basil, 2 tablespoons chopped parsley, the grated rind of 1 lemon and 1 small finely chopped clove of garlic.

cheat's curried vegetable soup

Serves **6**
Preparation time **25 minutes**
Cooking time **40 minutes**

2 tablespoons **sunflower oil**
1 **onion**, finely chopped
2 **garlic cloves**, finely chopped
4 teaspoons **ready-made mild curry paste**
2.5 cm (1 inch) piece of **fresh root ginger**, peeled, grated
2 small **baking potatoes**, diced
2 **carrots**, diced
1 small **cauliflower**, core discarded, florets cut into small pieces
75 g (3 oz) **red lentils**
1.5 litres (2½ pints) **vegetable or chicken stock** (see pages 13 and 10)
400 g (13 oz) can **chopped tomatoes**
200 g (7 oz) **spinach leaves**, rinsed and any large leaves torn into pieces

Raita
150 g (5 oz) **low-fat natural yogurt**
4 tablespoons chopped **coriander leaves**
4 teaspoons **mango chutney**

Heat the oil in a large saucepan, add the onion and fry for 5 minutes, stirring until softened. Stir in the garlic, curry paste and ginger and cook for 1 minute.

Mix in the potatoes, carrots, cauliflower and lentils. Pour in the stock and tomatoes, season with salt and pepper and bring to the boil. Cover and simmer for 30 minutes or until the lentils are tender.

Meanwhile, mix the yogurt, coriander and mango chutney together to make the raita and spoon into a small bowl.

Add the spinach to the soup and cook for 2 minutes until just wilted. Taste and adjust the seasoning if needed. Ladle the soup into shallow bowls, top with spoonfuls of raita. Serve with warmed naan breads, if liked.

For curried aubergine soup, fry the onion with 2 diced aubergines until the aubergines are lightly browned. Stir in the garlic, curry paste and ginger and cook as above. Add the potatoes, carrots, lentils, stock and tomatoes, omitting the cauliflower. After 30 minutes simmering, purée the soup in a blender or food processor then reheat. Omit the spinach, serve with a swirl of natural yogurt, a little chopped coriander and poppadums.

red pepper & courgette soup

Serves **4**
Preparation time **15 minutes**
Cooking time **about 40
  minutes**

2 tablespoons **olive oil**
2 **onions,** finely chopped
1 **garlic clove,** crushed
3 **red peppers,** cored,
  deseeded and roughly
  chopped
2 **courgettes,** roughly
  chopped
900 ml (1½ pints) **vegetable
  stock** (see page 13) or
  water
salt and **pepper**

To serve
low-fat natural yogurt or
  crème fraîche
whole chives

Heat the oil in a large saucepan and fry the onions gently for 5 minutes, or until softened and golden brown. Add the garlic and cook gently for 1 minute. Add the peppers and half the courgettes to the pan. Fry for 5–8 minutes, or until softened and brown.

Add the stock to the pan, season to taste with salt and pepper and bring to the boil. Reduce the heat, cover the pan and simmer gently for 20 minutes.

Allow the soup to cool slightly once the vegetables are tender, then purée in batches in a blender or food processor. Gently fry the remaining chopped courgette for 5 minutes. Meanwhile, return the soup to the pan, reheat, taste and adjust the seasoning if needed. Serve topped with the fried courgette, yogurt or crème fraîche and chives.

For red pepper & carrot soup, make up the soup as above, adding 2 diced carrots instead of the courgettes, plus the peppers to the fried onion and garlic. Continue as above. Purée, reheat and serve topped with 8 teaspoonfuls of garlic and herb soft cheese and some chopped chives.

fennel seed root vegetable soup

Serves **6**
Preparation time **25 minutes**
Cooking time **about 50 minutes**

1 tablespoon **olive oil**
1 **onion**, roughly chopped
2 **garlic cloves**, roughly chopped
2 teaspoons **fennel seeds**, roughly crushed
½ teaspoon **smoked paprika**
½ teaspoon **turmeric**
250 g (8 oz) **carrots**, diced
250 g (8 oz) **parsnips**, diced
250 g (8 oz) **swede**, diced
1 litre (1¾ pints) **vegetable** or **chicken stock** (see pages 13 and 10)
300 ml (½ pint) **skimmed milk**
salt and **pepper**

Heat the oil in a large saucepan, add the onion and fry for 5 minutes until just beginning to soften. Stir in the garlic, fennel seeds and spices and cook for 1 minute to release their flavour.

Add the root vegetables, stock, salt and pepper and bring to the boil. Cover and simmer for 45 minutes, stirring occasionally until the vegetables are very tender. Allow to cool slightly, then purée in batches in a blender or food processor until smooth.

Pour the purée back into the saucepan and stir in the milk. Reheat then taste and adjust the seasoning if needed. Ladle into bowls and serve with croûtons (see page 15).

For low-fat spiced croûtons, to serve as an accompaniment, cut 3 slices of wholemeal bread into cubes, put on a baking sheet, squirt with spray olive oil 3 or 4 times, then sprinkle with 1 teaspoon roughly crushed fennel seeds, ¼ teaspoon smoked paprika and ¼ teaspoon turmeric. Bake in a preheated oven set to 190°C (375°F), Gas Mark 5, for 15 minutes until crisp.

tomato & orange soup

Serves **6**
Preparation time **15 minutes**
Cooking time **about 40 minutes**

2 tablespoons **olive oil**
1 **onion**, roughly chopped
2 **garlic cloves**, crushed
2 kg (4 lb) **ripe tomatoes**, skinned and chopped
2 tablespoons **tomato purée**
450 ml (¾ pint) **vegetable** or **chicken stock** (see pages 13 and 10)
grated rind of 1 large **orange**
75 ml (3 fl oz) **orange juice**
4 **basil sprigs**
1–2 teaspoons **brown sugar**
salt and **pepper**

To garnish
2–3 tablespoons finely chopped **basil**
150 ml (¼ pint) **low-fat Greek yogurt**
6 small **basil sprigs**
thin strips of **orange rind**

Heat the oil in a large saucepan and fry the onion and garlic until softened. Add the tomatoes, tomato purée, stock, orange rind and juice and basil. Bring to the boil, then reduce the heat, cover the pan and simmer gently for 20–25 minutes until the vegetables are soft.

Allow the soup to cool slightly, then purée in batches in a blender or food processor and push through a nylon sieve into the rinsed pan to remove the seeds. Season with salt, pepper and a little sugar. Return the pan to the heat and bring to the boil, then add a little extra stock or tomato juice if necessary to achieve the desired consistency.

Fold the chopped basil gently into the Greek yogurt. Pour the hot soup into warmed soup plates, spoon a little basil yogurt on each one and garnish with small basil sprigs and orange rind.

For tomato soup with crispy chorizo, make up the soup as above, omitting the orange rind and juice, adding 75 ml (3 fl oz) red wine instead. Purée and serve topped with 40 g (1½ oz) ready sliced chorizo, dry fried until browned, then diced.

cauliflower & cumin soup

Serves **4**
Preparation time **15 minutes**
Cooking time **about 20 minutes**

2 teaspoons **sunflower oil**
1 **onion**, chopped
1 **garlic clove**, crushed
2 teaspoons **cumin seeds**
1 **cauliflower**, cut into florets
1 large **potato**, peeled and chopped
450 ml (¾ pint) **vegetable stock** (see page 13)
450 ml (¾ pint) **semi-skimmed milk**
2 tablespoons **low-fat crème fraîche**
2 tablespoons chopped **coriander leaves**
salt and **pepper**

Heat the oil in a medium saucepan and fry the onion, garlic and cumin seeds for 3–4 minutes. Add the cauliflower, potato, stock and milk and bring to the boil. Reduce the heat and simmer for 15 minutes.

Transfer the soup to a blender or food processor and purée until smooth. Stir through the crème fraîche and coriander and season to taste with salt and pepper. Heat through and serve with slices of crusty wholemeal bread.

For curried cauliflower soup, fry the onion and garlic in the oil as above, omitting the cumin. Stir in 2 tablespoons mild curry paste, cook for 1 minute then add the cauliflower, potato, stock and milk. Continue as the recipe above. Serve with some tiny circular poppadums.

fennel & lemon soup

Serves **4**
Preparation time **20 minutes**
Cooking time **about 25 minutes**

50 ml (2 fl oz) **olive oil**
3 large **spring onions**, chopped
250 g (8 oz) **fennel bulb**, trimmed, cored and finely sliced
1 **potato**, peeled and diced
finely grated rind and juice of **1 lemon**
900 ml (1½ pints) **chicken** or **vegetable stock** (see pages 10 and 13)
salt and **pepper**

Black olive gremolata
1 small **garlic clove**, finely chopped
finely grated rind of **1 lemon**
4 tablespoons chopped **parsley**
16 **black Greek olives**, pitted and chopped

Heat the oil in a large saucepan and fry the spring onions for 5 minutes until soft. Add the fennel, potato and lemon rind and cook for 5 minutes until the fennel begins to soften. Pour in the stock and bring to the boil. Reduce the heat, cover the pan and simmer for about 15 minutes until the ingredients are tender.

Meanwhile, to make the gremolata, mix together the garlic, lemon rind and parsley, then stir in the olives. Cover and chill until required.

Purée the soup in a blender or food processor and pass it through a sieve to remove any strings of fennel. The soup should not be too thick, so add more stock if necessary. Return the soup to the rinsed pan. Taste and season well with salt and pepper and lemon juice, then heat through gently. Pour the soup into warmed bowls and sprinkle with some gremolata, to be stirred in before eating. Serve with slices of toasted crusty bread, or croûtons (see page 15), if liked.

For fennel & trout soup, omit the gremolata and instead steam 2 boneless trout fillets above the simmering soup for 10 minutes, until the fish flakes easily when pressed with a knife. Lift the trout out of the steamer, remove the skin then break into flakes, removing any bones. Spoon into the base of 4 shallow serving bowls then ladle the soup over the top.

roast root vegetable soup

Serves **6**

Preparation time **10 minutes**

Cooking time **1 hour 5 minutes**

4 **carrots**, chopped

2 **parsnips**, chopped

olive oil, for spraying

1 **leek**, finely chopped

1.2 litres (2 pints) **vegetable stock** (see page 13)

2 teaspoons **thyme leaves**

salt and **pepper**

thyme sprigs, to garnish

Place the carrots and parsnips in a roasting tin, spray lightly with olive oil and season with salt and pepper. Roast in a preheated oven, 200°C (400°F), Gas Mark 6, for 1 hour or until the vegetables are very soft.

Meanwhile, 20 minutes before the vegetables have finished roasting, put the leeks in a large saucepan with the stock and 1 teaspoon of the thyme. Cover the pan and simmer for 20 minutes.

Transfer the roasted root vegetables to a blender or food processor and blend, adding a little of the stock if necessary. Transfer to the stock saucepan and season to taste. Add the remaining thyme, stir and simmer for 5 minutes to reheat.

Ladle into individual bowls and serve garnished with the thyme sprigs.

For roast butternut squash soup, halve, deseed then peel a 750 g (1 ½ lb) butternut squash, cut into thick slices and put into a roasting tin. Spray with a little olive oil and season with salt and pepper. Roast at 200°C (400°F), Gas Mark 6, for 45 minutes then continue as the recipe above.

red pepper & ginger soup

Serves **4**

Preparation time **20 minutes**,
  plus cooling

Cooking time **45 minutes**

3 **red peppers**, halved, cored
  and deseeded
1 **red onion**, quartered
2 **garlic cloves**
1 teaspoon **olive oil**
5 cm (2 inches) piece of **fresh
  root ginger**, grated
1 teaspoon **ground cumin**
1 teaspoon **ground coriander**
1 large **potato**, chopped
900 ml (1½ pints) **vegetable
  stock** (see page 13)
4 tablespoons **fromage frais**
salt and **pepper**

Place the peppers, onion and garlic cloves in a nonstick roasting tin. Roast in a preheated oven, 200°C (400°F), Gas Mark 6, for 40 minutes or until the peppers have blistered and the onion quarters and garlic are soft. If the onion quarters start to brown too much, cover them with the pepper halves and continue cooking.

Meanwhile, heat the oil in a saucepan and fry the ginger, cumin and coriander over a low heat for 5 minutes until softened. Add the potato, stir well and season to taste with salt and pepper. Add the stock, cover the pan and simmer for 30 minutes.

Remove the roasted vegetables from the oven. Place the peppers in a polythene bag, tie the top and leave to cool. Add the onions to the potato mixture and carefully squeeze out the garlic pulp from the skins into the saucepan. Remove the skins from the peppers and add all but one half to the soup. Simmer for 5 minutes.

Purée the soup in a food processor or blender until smooth. Return to the saucepan and thin with a little water, if necessary, to achieve the desired consistency.

Spoon into individual bowls. Slice the remaining piece of pepper and place the strips on top of the soup with a spoonful of fromage frais.

For red pepper & pesto soup, roast the peppers, onion and garlic as above. Heat the oil in a saucepan, omit the spices and add 2 teaspoons pesto sauce and the diced potato, fry gently for 2–3 minutes then continue as the recipe above.

courgette & dill soup

Serves **8**

Preparation time **20 minutes**

Cooking time **20–25 minutes**

2 tablespoons **sunflower** or **light olive oil**

1 large **onion**, chopped

2 **garlic cloves**, crushed

1 kg (2 lb) **courgettes**, sliced

1.2–1.5 litres (2–2½) pints **vegetable** or **chicken stock** (see pages 13 and 10)

2–4 tablespoons finely chopped **dill**

salt and **pepper**

To garnish

125 ml (4 fl oz) **single cream**

dill fronds

Heat the oil in a saucepan and fry the onion and garlic until soft but not browned. Add the courgettes, cover the pan with greaseproof paper and cook over a low heat for 10 minutes until the courgettes are soft. Add 1.2 litres (2 pints) of the stock, cover the pan with a lid and simmer for a further 10–15 minutes.

Transfer the courgettes and a little of the stock to a blender or food processor. Purée until smooth, then pour into a clean saucepan. Add the stock that the courgettes were cooked in and the remaining stock, along with the chopped dill. Season to taste with salt and pepper, then bring to the boil.

Serve the soup in warmed soup bowls, garnished with a swirl of cream and dill fronds.

For mixed squash & dill soup, heat 2 tablespoons sunflower oil in a saucepan, add 1 chopped onion and 2 crushed garlic cloves and fry for 5 minutes. Add 500 g (1 lb) diced courgettes or marrow and 500 g (1 lb) prepared and diced pumpkin or butternut squash (weigh after deseeding and peeling). Cook gently as above, then add the stock and continue as above. Serve with garlic croûtons (see page 15).

bean & sun-dried tomato soup

Serves **4**
Preparation time **5 minutes**
Cooking time **20 minutes**

3 tablespoons **extra virgin
  olive oil**
1 **onion**, finely chopped
2 **celery sticks**, thinly sliced
2 **garlic cloves**, thinly sliced
2 x 425 g (14 oz) cans **butter
  beans**, drained and rinsed
4 tablespoons **sun-dried
  tomato paste**
900 ml (1½ pints) **vegetable
  stock** (see page 13)
1 tablespoon chopped
  rosemary or **thyme**
salt and **pepper**
Parmesan cheese shavings,
  to garnish

Heat the oil in a saucepan. Add the onion and fry for
3 minutes until softened. Add the celery and garlic and
fry for 2 minutes.

Add the butter beans, sun-dried tomato paste,
vegetable stock, rosemary or thyme and a little salt and
pepper. Bring to the boil, then reduce the heat, cover
and simmer gently for 15 minutes. Serve sprinkled with
Parmesan shavings.

For chickpea, tomato & rosemary soup, stir

2 x 425 g (14 oz) cans of drained chickpeas into the
fried onion, celery and garlic mixture. Add 3 tablespoons
ordinary tomato purée, 2 teaspoons harissa paste,
900 ml (1½ pints) vegetable stock and 1 tablespoon
fresh chopped rosemary leaves. Cover, simmer and
serve as above.

spicy coriander & lentil soup

Serves **8**
Preparation time **10–15
minutes**
Cooking time **40–50 minutes**

500 g (1 lb) **red lentils**
2 tablespoons **vegetable oil**
2 **onions**, chopped
2 **garlic cloves**, chopped
2 **celery sticks**, chopped
400 g (13 oz) can **tomatoes**,
    drained
1 **chilli**, deseeded and
    chopped (optional)
1 teaspoon **paprika**
1 teaspoon **harissa paste**
1 teaspoon **ground cumin**
1.2 litres (2 pints) **vegetable
    stock** (see page 13)
salt and **pepper**
2 tablespoons chopped
    coriander, to garnish

Place the lentils in a bowl of water. Heat the oil in a large saucepan and gently fry the onions, garlic and celery over a low heat until softened.

Drain the lentils and add them to the vegetable pan with the tomatoes. Mix well. Add the chilli, if using, paprika, harissa paste, cumin and vegetable stock and season with salt and pepper. Cover the pan and simmer gently for about 40–50 minutes until the lentils are tender, adding a little more vegetable stock or water if the soup gets too thick.

Serve the soup immediately in warmed individual bowls topped with a little chopped coriander.

For spicy coriander & white bean soup, fry
the onions, garlic and celery in the oil as above. Drain 2 x 425 g (14 oz) cans of haricot or cannellini beans then add to the pan with chilli, flavourings and stock as above. Simmer for 40–50 minutes then roughly mash some of the beans to thicken the soup. Finish with 2 tablespoons fresh chopped coriander and 4 tablespoons fresh chopped parsley.

summer green pea soup

Serves **4**

Preparation time **10 minutes or longer if shelling fresh peas**

Cooking time **about 15 minutes**

1 tablespoon **butter**

bunch of **spring onions**, chopped

1.25 kg (2½ lb) **fresh peas**, shelled, or 500 g (1 lb) **frozen peas**

750 ml (1¼ pints) **vegetable stock** (see page 13)

2 tablespoons **thick natural yogurt** or **single cream**

nutmeg

1 tablespoon chopped and 2 whole **chives**, to garnish

Melt the butter in a large pan and soften the onions, but do not allow them to colour. Add the peas to the pan with the stock. Bring to the boil and simmer for about 5 minutes for frozen peas, but for up to 15 minutes for fresh peas, until they are cooked. Be careful not to overcook fresh peas or they will lose their flavour.

Remove from the heat and purée in a blender or food processor. Add the yogurt or cream and grate in a little nutmeg. Reheat gently if necessary, and serve sprinkled with chives.

For minted pea & broad bean soup, fry the spring onions in the butter as above then add 625 g (1¼ lb) fresh peas and 625 g (1¼ lb) fresh broad beans, both podded or 250 g (8 oz) frozen peas and 250 g (8 oz) frozen broad beans, 2 stems of fresh mint and the stock. Simmer as above then purée, reheat and ladle into bowls, top with 4 tablespoons double cream, swirled into the soup and a few tiny fresh mint leaves.

scallop & broccoli broth

Serves **4**
Preparation time **10 minutes**
Cooking time **about 40 minutes**

1.2 litres (2 pints) **vegetable or chicken stock** (see pages 13 and 10)
25 g (1 oz) **fresh root ginger**, peeled and cut into thin strips, peel reserved
1 tablespoon **soy sauce**
3 **spring onions**, cut into fine diagonal slices
500 g (1 lb) **broccoli**, trimmed and cut into small florets
1 small **red chilli**, deseeded and finely sliced (optional)
12 large **scallops**, with roes
few drops of **Thai fish sauce**
juice of ½ **lime**
sesame oil, to serve

Put the stock into a large saucepan with the ginger peel and boil for 15 minutes. Set aside and allow to steep for a further 15 minutes.

Strain the stock into a clean saucepan. Add the soy sauce, strips of ginger, spring onions, broccoli and chilli, if using, and simmer for 5 minutes.

Add the scallops, simmer for a further 3 minutes, or until the scallops are just cooked through. Season with Thai fish sauce and lime juice.

Remove the scallops from the soup with a slotted spoon and put 3 in each individual soup bowl. Divide the broccoli among the bowls and pour in the hot soup. Serve immediately with a few drops of sesame oil.

For mixed seafood & broccoli broth, make up the broth as above but omitting the scallops. Tip a 200 g (7 oz) frozen mixed bag of seafood including sliced squid, mussels and prawns that has been thoroughly defrosted into a sieve, rinse with cold water, drain again and then add to the broth. Simmer for 3–4 minutes until piping hot then ladle into bowls.

around the world

scottish cullen skink

Serves **6**
Preparation time **25 minutes**
Cooking time **40 minutes**

25 g (1 oz) **butter**
1 **onion**, roughly chopped
500 g (1 lb) **potatoes**, diced
1 large **Finnan haddock** or
   300 g (10 oz) **smoked
   haddock fillet**
1 **bay leaf**
900 ml (1½ pint) **fish stock**
   (see page 13)
150 ml (¼ pints) **milk**
6 tablespoons **double cream**
salt and **pepper**
chopped **parsley**, to garnish

Heat the butter in a saucepan, add the onion and fry gently for 5 minutes until softened. Stir the potatoes into the butter and onion then cover and cook for 5 more minutes. Lay the haddock on top, add the bay leaf and stock. Season with salt and pepper and bring to the boil.

Cover and simmer for 30 minutes or until the potatoes are soft. Lift the fish out of the pan with a slotted spoon and transfer to a plate. Discard the bay leaf.

Loosen the bones, if using a Finnan haddock, with a small knife, then lift away the backbone and head. Using a knife and fork break the fish into flakes and lift off the skin. If using haddock fillet, simply peel off the skin and then break the fish into flakes, double-checking there are no bones. Return two thirds of the fish to the pan then purée the soup in batches in a blender or food processor until smooth. Pour back into the saucepan and stir in the milk and cream. Bring just to the boil, then simmer gently until reheated. Taste and adjust the seasoning if needed.

Ladle into bowls, sprinkle with the remaining fish and the chopped parsley. Serve with toasted barley bannocks or soda griddle scones.

For Scottish ham & haddie bree, add 6 rashers diced smoked streaky bacon when frying the potato until it is just beginning to turn golden. Add the fish, bay leaf, stock and seasoning and simmer gently as above. Lift the fish out of the soup and flake then return to the soup with the milk and cream and serve as a chunky soup topped with chopped chives.

cajun red bean soup

Serves **6**

Preparation time **25 minutes, plus overnight soaking**

Cooking time **1 hour**

2 tablespoons **sunflower oil**

1 large **onion**, chopped

1 **red pepper**, halved, cored and diced

1 **carrot**, diced

1 **baking potato**, diced

2–3 **garlic cloves**, chopped (optional)

2 teaspoons **mixed Cajun spice**

400 g (13 oz) can **chopped tomatoes**

1 tablespoon **brown sugar**

1 litre (1¾ pints) **vegetable stock** (see page 13)

425 g (14 oz) can **red kidney beans**, drained

50 g (2 oz) **okra**, sliced

50 g (2 oz) **green beans**, thinly sliced

salt and **pepper**

Heat the oil in a large frying pan. Add the onion and fry for 5 minutes until softened. Add the red pepper, carrot, potato and garlic, if using, and fry for 5 minutes. Stir in the mixed Cajun spice, tomatoes, sugar, stock and plenty of salt and pepper and bring to the boil.

Add the drained beans and mix together. Bring to the boil, then cover and simmer for 45 minutes until the vegetables are tender.

Add the sliced green vegetables, re-cover and cook for 5 minutes until just cooked. Ladle the soup into bowls and serve with crusty bread.

For Hungarian paprika & red bean soup, make up the soup as above adding 1 teaspoon of paprika instead of the Cajun spice. Simmer for 45 minutes, omit the green vegetables then purée and reheat. Ladle into bowls and serve topped with 2 tablespoons of soured cream and a few caraway seeds.

seafood & corn chowder

Serves **6**
Preparation time **40 minutes**
Cooking time **35 minutes**

25 g (1 oz) **butter**
½ bunch of **spring onions**,
   trimmed, sliced, white and
   green parts kept separate
200 g (7 oz) **potatoes**, diced
300 ml (½ pint) **fish stock**
   (see page 13)
1 large **bay leaf**
150 g (5 oz) **smoked
   haddock**
150 g (5 oz) **haddock** or **cod**
50 g (2 oz) **frozen sweetcorn**
200 g (7 oz) **frozen seafood
   selection**, defrosted, rinsed
   and drained
300 ml (½ pint) **milk**
150 ml (¼ pint) **double
   cream**
2 tablespoons fresh chopped
   parsley
salt and **pepper**
6 large **bread rolls**, tops
   sliced off and centres
   hollowed out to make a
   bread casing (optional)

Heat the butter in a saucepan, add the white sliced spring onions and the potato, toss in the butter then cover and fry gently for 10 minutes, stirring occasionally until only just beginning to colour.

Pour in the stock, add the bay leaf then lay the fish fillets on top and season with salt and pepper. Bring to the boil then cover and simmer gently for 20 minutes until the potatoes are tender. Lift the fish out of the soup with a slotted spoon, put on a plate and peel away the skin. Flake into pieces, carefully checking for any bones.

Return the fish to the saucepan, add the green spring onions tops, the frozen sweetcorn, defrosted shellfish and milk. Bring back to the boil then cover and simmer for 5 minutes until the seafood is reheated. Discard the bay leaf. Pour in the cream, add the parsley then taste and adjust the seasoning if needed. Bring back to the boil then ladle into hollowed out bread rolls. Scoop out the soup with a small spoon then eat the bread last when steeped in all the fishy flavours.

For chicken & corn chowder, add the diced meat of 6 small skinned and boned chicken thighs to the white spring onions and fry for 5 minutes until just turning golden. Add 200 g (7 oz) diced potato then cover and fry gently for 5 minutes. Pour in 300 ml (½ pint) chicken stock, add 1 large bay leaf and seasoning. Cover and simmer gently for 30 minutes. Add the green spring onion slices, frozen sweetcorn, 50 g (2 oz) diced cooked ham and the milk. Simmer gently for 5 minutes then mix in the double cream. Serve in bread rolls or bowls.

vietnamese beef pho

Serves **6**
Preparation time **15 minutes**
Cooking time **about 45 minutes**

1 teaspoon **sunflower oil**
1 teaspoon **Szechuan peppercorns**, roughly crushed
1 **lemon grass stem**, sliced
1 **cinnamon stick**, broken into pieces
2 **star anise**
4 cm (1½ inch) piece of **fresh root ginger**, peeled, sliced
small bunch of **coriander**
1.5 litres (2½ pints) **beef stock** (see page 12)
1 tablespoon **fish sauce**
juice of **1 lime**
100 g (3½ oz) **fine rice noodles**
250 g (8 oz) **rump or flash-fry beef steak**, fat trimmed, meat thinly sliced
100 g (3½ oz) **bean sprouts**, rinsed
4 **spring onions**, thinly sliced
1 large **mild red chilli**, thinly sliced

Heat the oil in a saucepan, add the peppercorns, lemon grass, cinnamon, star anise and ginger and cook for 1 minute to release their flavours. Cut the stems from the coriander and add the stems to the pan with the stock. Bring to the boil, stirring then cover and simmer for 40 minutes.

Strain the stock and return to the pan. Stir in the fish sauce and lime juice. Cook the noodles in a pan of boiling water as directed on the pack then drain and divide between 6 small bowls. Add the steak to the soup and cook for 1–2 minutes. Divide the bean sprouts, spring onions and chilli between the bowls then ladle the soup on top and finish with the remaining coriander leaves, torn into pieces.

For Vietnamese prawn soup, make up the flavoured broth as above, using 1.5 litres (2½ pints) chicken or vegetable stock (see pages 10 and 13) and 2 kaffir lime leaves instead of the cinnamon. Simmer for 40 minutes then drain and finish as above, adding 200 g (7 oz) raw peeled prawns and 150 g (5 oz) sliced button mushrooms instead of the steak, cook for 4–5 minutes until the prawns are pink. Finish with bean sprouts, spring onions and chilli as above.

greek chicken avgolomeno

Serves **6**

Preparation time **10 minutes**

Cooking time **15–20 minutes**

2 litres (3½ pints) **chicken stock** (see page 10)

125 g (4 oz) **orzo, macaroni or other small pasta shapes**

25 g (1 oz) **butter**

25 g (1 oz) **plain flour**

4 **egg yolks**

grated rind and juice of 1 **lemon**

salt and **pepper**

To garnish (optional)

125 g (4 oz) cooked **chicken**, torn into fine shreds

extra **lemon rind**

oregano leaves

lemon wedges

Bring the stock to the boil, add the pasta and simmer for 8–10 minutes until just tender. Meanwhile heat the butter in a separate smaller pan, stir in the flour then gradually mix in 2 ladlefuls of the stock from the large pan. Bring to the boil, stirring. Take off the heat.

Mix the egg yolks in a medium-sized bowl with the lemon rind and some salt and pepper. Gradually mix in the lemon juice until smooth. Slowly mix in the hot sauce from the small pan, stirring continuously.

Stir a couple more hot ladlefuls of stock into the lemon mixture once the pasta is cooked, then pour this into the large pasta pan. (Don't be tempted to add the eggs and lemon straight into the pasta pan or it may curdle.) Mix well, then ladle into shallow soup bowls and top with shredded chicken taken off the carcass, some extra lemon rind and some torn oregano leaves. Serve with lemon wedges.

For cod avgolomeno, bring 2 litres (3½ pints) strained fish stock to the boil in a large saucepan, add 125 g (4 oz) small pasta shapes and 625 g (1¼ lb) skinned cod fillet, simmer for 8–10 minutes until both are tender. Break the fish into flakes, discarding the skin and any bones. Make the sauce with the butter and flour as above then mix in some of the stock, the egg yolks and lemon mix. Add this to the pasta and fish, then ladle into bowls and top with snipped chives or a little snipped chervil.

mushroom hot & sour soup

Serves **4–6**

Preparation time **5–10 minutes**

Cooking time **about 15 minutes**

1.2 litres (2 pints) **fish stock** (see page 13)

1 **lemon grass stalk**, lightly bruised

3 **dried kaffir lime leaves** or 3 pieces of **lime peel**

2 **Thai red chillies**, halved and deseeded

2 tablespoons **lime juice**

1–2 tablespoons **Thai fish sauce**

50 g (2 oz) **canned bamboo shoots**

125 g (4 oz) **oyster mushrooms**

2 **spring onions**, finely sliced

½ **red chilli**, sliced, to garnish

Pour the fish stock into a saucepan, add the lemon grass, lime leaves or peel and chillies. Simmer for 10 minutes. Strain the liquid into a clean saucepan. Reserve a little of the red chilli from the sieve and discard the remaining seasonings.

Add the lime juice and fish sauce to taste to the stock with the bamboo shoots, mushrooms and reserved chilli. Simmer for 5 minutes. Ladle the soup into individual bowls and sprinkle with the spring onions. Garnish with fresh red chilli slices.

For vegetarian tomato hot & sour soup, make the soup following the method above, but use 1.2 litres (2 pints) of vegetable stock (see page 13) in place of the fish stock, and use 2 tablespoons light soy sauce in place of the fish sauce. Stir in 4 skinned, deseeded and chopped tomatoes and 1 ½ deseeded and diced red peppers instead of the mushrooms.

italian tortellini in brodo

Serves **6**
Preparation time **10 minutes**
Cooking time **about 10
  minutes**

500 g (1 lb) **tomatoes**
1.5 litres (2½ pints) **chicken
  stock** (see page 10)
200 ml (7 fl oz) **dry white
  wine**
1 tablespoon **sun-dried
  tomato paste**
small bunch **basil**, roughly torn
  into pieces
300 g (10 oz) pack **spinach
  and ricotta tortellini**, or
  filling of your choice
6 tablespoons freshly grated
  Parmesan cheese, plus
  extra to serve
salt and **pepper**

Make a cross cut in the base of each tomato, put into
a bowl and cover with boiling water. Leave to soak for
1 minute, then drain and peel away the skins. Quarter
the tomatoes, scoop out the seeds and dice the flesh.

Put the tomatoes into a saucepan, add the stock, wine
and tomato paste, season with salt and pepper and
bring to the boil. Simmer gently for 5 minutes.

Add half the basil and all the pasta, bring back to the
boil and cook for 3–4 minutes until the pasta is just
cooked. Stir in the Parmesan, taste and adjust the
seasoning if needed. Ladle into bowls, serve with a
little extra grated Parmesan and garnish with the
remaining basil leaves.

For gnocchi & pesto broth, flavour 1.5 litres (2½ pints)
chicken stock with tomatoes, wine and sun-dried
tomato paste as above. Add 2 tablespoons pesto and
bring to the boil. Add 300 g (10 oz) chilled gnocchi
instead of tortellini and 125 g (4 oz) shredded spinach,
simmer for 5 minutes until the gnocchi rise to the
surface and the spinach has wilted. Stir in the freshly
grated Parmesan and finish as above.

hungarian chorba

Serves **6**
Preparation time **25 minutes**
Cooking time **2½ hours**

1 tablespoon **sunflower oil**
500 g (1 lb) **stewing lamb on the bone**
1 **onion**, finely chopped
1 **carrot**, roughly chopped
150 g (5 oz) **swede**, roughly chopped
2 teaspoons **smoked paprika**
50 g (2 oz) **long-grain rice**
small bunch **dill**, plus extra, torn, to garnish
1.5 litres (2½ pints) **lamb stock** (see page 12)
4–6 tablespoons **red wine vinegar**
2 tablespoons **brown sugar**
2 **eggs**
salt and **pepper**

Heat the oil in a large saucepan, add the lamb and brown on one side, turn over and add the onion, carrot and swede and cook until both sides of the lamb are browned.

Sprinkle over the paprika, cook briefly then add the rice, dill and lamb stock. Spoon in the vinegar, sugar and plenty of salt and pepper then bring to the boil, stirring. Cover and simmer for 2½ hours until the lamb is very tender.

Lift the lamb out of the saucepan with a slotted spoon, transfer to a chopping board and cut the meat into small pieces, discarding the bones and fat. Return the lamb to the pan. Beat the eggs in a bowl, gradually mix in a ladleful of hot soup then pour into the saucepan. Heat gently until the soup has thickened slightly, but do not boil or the eggs will scramble. Taste and adjust the seasoning and vinegar if needed. Garnish with extra torn dill and ladle into bowls. Serve with sliced pumpernickel bread.

For chicken & kohlrabi chorba, fry 6 chicken thighs in place of the lamb. Add the onion and carrot and then add 150 g (5 oz) peeled and diced kohlrabi in place of the swede. Continue as above, simmering for just 1½ hours.

thai prawn broth

Serves **4**

Preparation time **15 minutes**

Cooking time **about 10 minutes**

1.2 litres (2 pints) **vegetable stock** (see page 13)

2 teaspoons **ready-made Thai red curry paste**

4 dried **kaffir lime leaves**, torn into pieces

3–4 teaspoons **Thai fish sauce**

2 **spring onions**, sliced

150 g (5 oz) **shiitake mushrooms**, sliced

125 g (4 oz) **dried soba (Japanese) noodles**

½ **red pepper**, cored, deseeded and diced

125 g (4 oz) **pak choi**, thinly sliced

250 g (8 oz) **frozen prawns**, defrosted and rinsed

small bunch of **coriander leaves**, torn into pieces

Pour the stock into a saucepan, add the curry paste, lime leaves, fish sauce to taste, spring onions and mushrooms. Bring to the boil and simmer for 5 minutes.

Bring a separate pan of water to the boil, add the noodles and cook for 3 minutes.

Add the remaining ingredients to the soup and cook for 2 minutes until piping hot.

Drain the noodles, rinse with fresh hot water and spoon into the base of 4 bowls. Ladle the hot prawn broth over the top and serve immediately with small bowls of Thai fish sauce and dark soy sauce for seasoning, if liked.

For Thai tamarind broth, put the stock into a pan, add 2 teaspoons tamarind concentrate and ¼ teaspoon turmeric, then the curry paste and flavourings as above. Simmer for 5 minutes and continue as above, omitting the prawns.

chicken soup with lockshen

Serves **6**
Preparation time **20 minutes**
Cooking time **5 minutes**

2 litres (3½ pints) **chicken stock** (see page 10)
150–200 g (5–7 oz) cooked, shredded **chicken**
100 g (3½ oz) **lockshen** (vermicelli pasta)
salt and **pepper**
chopped **parsley**, to garnish (optional)

Bring the stock to the boil in a large saucepan, add the shredded chicken and heat thoroughly. Meanwhile, bring a second pan of water to the boil, add the lockshen and simmer for 4–5 minutes until tender.

Drain the lockshen, divide it between soup bowls, so that it makes a small nest in the base of each, then ladle the soup on top. Garnish with a little parsley, if liked.

For chicken soup with kneidlech, make up the soup as above, omitting the lockshen. Put 125 g (4 oz) medium matzo meal into a bowl with a pinch of ground ginger, salt and pepper and 1 beaten egg. Add 1 tablespoon melted schmalz (chicken fat available from Kosher butchers) or non-dairy margarine then mix in 5–6 tablespoons of hot chicken stock or water to make a mouldable dough. Divide into 20, shape into small balls and chill on a plate for 1 hour. Add to a saucepan of simmering water and cook for 25 minutes until they rise to the surface of the water and are spongy. Drain well and add to bowls of the chicken soup.

ghanaian groundnut soup

Serves **6**

Preparation time **15 minutes**

Cooking time **about 40 minutes**

1 tablespoon **sunflower oil**

1 **onion**, finely chopped

2 **carrots**, diced

500 g (1 lb) **tomatoes**, skinned if liked, roughly chopped

½ teaspoon **piri piri seasoning** or **crushed chilli flakes**

100 g (3½ oz) **roasted salted peanuts**

1 litre (1¾ pints) **fish** or **vegetable stock** (see page 13)

To garnish

crushed chilli flakes

peanuts, roughly chopped

Heat the oil in a saucepan, add the onion and carrot and fry for 5 minutes, stirring until softened and just turning golden around the edges. Stir in the tomatoes and piri piri and cook for 1 minute.

Grind the peanuts in a spice mill or liquidizer until you have a fine powder like ground almonds. Stir into the tomatoes, add the stock and then bring to the boil. Cover and simmer for 30 minutes. Mash or purée half the soup and reheat. Taste and adjust the seasoning if needed, then ladle into bowls, garnish with crushed chilli flakes and peanuts and serve with foo foo (see below).

For homemade foo foo, to serve as an accompaniment, peel and cut 750 g (1½ lb) yam or potatoes into chunks and cook in a saucepan of boiling water for 20 minutes until tender. Drain and mash with 3 tablespoons milk and seasoning. Shape into balls and serve separately for dunking into the hot soup.

chicken mulligatawny

Serves **6**
Preparation time **15 minutes**
Cooking time **about 1¼ hours**

1 tablespoon **sunflower oil**
1 **onion**, finely chopped
1 **carrot**, diced
1 **dessert apple**, peeled,
  cored and diced
2 **garlic cloves**, finely
  chopped
250 g (8 oz) **tomatoes**,
  skinned if liked, roughly
  chopped
4 teaspoons **medium curry
  paste**
50 g (2 oz) **sultanas**
125 g (4 oz) **red lentils**
1.5 litres (2½ pints) **chicken
  stock** (see page 10)
125 g (4 oz) **leftover cooked
  chicken**, cut into shreds
salt and **pepper**
coriander sprigs, to garnish

Heat the oil in a saucepan, add the onion and carrot and fry for 5 minutes, stirring until softened and just turning golden around the edges. Stir in the apple, garlic, tomatoes and curry paste and cook for 2 minutes.

Stir in the sultanas, lentils and stock. Season with salt and pepper and bring to the boil, cover and simmer for 1 hour until the lentils are soft. Mash the soup to make a coarse purée. Add the cooked chicken, heat thoroughly then taste and adjust the seasoning if needed. Ladle into bowls and garnish with coriander sprigs. Serve with warm naan bread or poppadums.

For citrus carrot mulligatawny, fry the onion with 500 g (1 lb) diced carrots in 2 tablespoons sunflower oil for 5 minutes. Omit the next five ingredients, then add the red lentils, the grated rind and juice of 1 orange and ½ lemon and 1.5 litres (2½ pints) vegetable stock (see page 13). Bring to the boil, cover and simmer for 1 hour. Purée until smooth then reheat and adjust seasoning. Serve with croûtons (see page 15).

london particular

Serves **6**
Preparation time **25 minutes**
plus soaking time
Cooking time **1 hour 20
minutes**

300 g (10 oz) **dried green
split peas**, soaked overnight
in cold water
25 g (1 oz) **butter**
4 **smoked streaky bacon
rashers**, diced
1 **onion**, roughly chopped
1 **carrot**, diced
2 **celery sticks**, diced
1.5 litres (2½ pints) **ham** or
chicken stock (see pages
10 and 11)
salt and **pepper**

To garnish
handful of **parsley**, chopped
4 **smoked streaky bacon
rashers**, grilled and snipped

Drain the peas into a colander. Heat the butter in a
large saucepan, add the bacon and onion and fry for
5 minutes until softened. Add the carrot and celery and
fry for 5 more minutes, stirring until golden.

Add the peas and stock and bring to the boil, stirring.
Boil rapidly for 10 minutes then reduce the heat, cover
and simmer for about 1 hour or until the peas are tender.

Allow the soup to cool slightly then purée half the
soup in batches in a blender or food processor until
smooth. Return to the saucepan and reheat. Add salt
and pepper to taste.

Ladle the soup into bowls then sprinkle the parsley
and bacon over the top.

For mixed pea broth, soak 300 g (10 oz) soup mix
(a blend of yellow and green split peas, pearl barley
and red lentils) in cold water overnight. Make up the
soup as above adding this instead of the soaked
green split peas. Serve topped with 4 slices bread cut
from a white bread roll, toasted then spread with 25 g
(1 oz) butter mixed with 2 teaspoons anchovy relish or
3 finely chopped and drained canned anchovies.

tomato & bread soup

Serves **4**
Preparation time **10 minutes**
Cooking time **35 minutes**

1 kg (2 lb) **really ripe vine
   tomatoes**, skinned,
   deseeded and chopped
300 ml (½ pint) **vegetable
   stock** (see page 13)
6 tablespoons **extra virgin
   olive oil**
2 **garlic cloves**, crushed
1 teaspoon **sugar**
2 tablespoons chopped **basil**
100 g (3½ oz) **ciabatta bread**
1 tablespoon **balsamic
   vinegar**
salt and **pepper**
basil leaves, to garnish

Place the tomatoes in a saucepan with the stock,
2 tablespoons of the oil, the garlic, sugar and basil and
gradually bring to the boil. Cover the pan and simmer
gently for 30 minutes.

Crumble the bread into the soup and stir over a low
heat until it has thickened. Stir in the vinegar and the
remaining oil and season with salt and pepper to
taste. Serve immediately or leave to cool to room
temperature, if preferred. Garnish with basil leaves.

For tomato & bread soup with roasted peppers,
halve 1 red and 1 orange pepper, scoop out the
seeds then put cut side downwards in a grill pan,
brush with 1 tablespoon of olive oil then grill for
10 minutes until the skins have charred. Wrap in foil
and cool. Peel off the skins and slice. Add to a
saucepan with 1.5 kg (3 lb) skinned and deseeded
tomatoes and the stock, oil, garlic, sugar and basil as
above. Bring to the boil then continue as above.

caribbean pepper pot soup

Serves **6**
Preparation time **20 minutes**
Cooking time **about 50 minutes**

2 tablespoons **olive oil**
1 **onion**, finely chopped
1 **Scotch bonnet chilli**, deseeded, finely chopped or 2 **hot Thai red chillies**, chopped with seeds
2 **red peppers**, cored, deseeded, diced
2 **garlic cloves**, finely chopped
1 large **carrot**, diced
200 g (7 oz) **potatoes**, diced
1 **bay leaf**
1 **thyme sprig**
400 ml (14 fl oz) can **full-fat coconut milk**
600 ml (1 pint) **beef stock** (see page 12)
salt and **cayenne pepper**

To garnish
200 g (7 oz) **rump steak**
2 teaspoons **olive oil**

Heat the oil in a saucepan, add the onion and fry gently for 5 minutes until softened and just beginning to turn golden. Stir in the chilli, red pepper, garlic, carrot, potato and herbs and fry for 5 minutes, stirring.

Pour in the coconut milk and beef stock, then season with salt and cayenne pepper. Bring to the boil, stirring, then cover and simmer for 30 minutes or until the vegetables are tender. Discard the herbs, then taste and adjust the seasoning if needed.

Rub the steak with the oil then season lightly with salt and cayenne pepper. Heat a griddle or frying pan and when hot add the steak and fry for 2–5 minutes on each side to taste. Leave to stand for 5 minutes then slice thinly. Ladle the soup into bowls, garnish with the steak slices and serve with crusty bread.

For prawn & spinach pepper pot soup, make
up the soup as above using 600 ml (1 pint) fish stock (see page 13) in place of the beef stock. Simmer for 30 minutes, then add 200 g (7 oz) raw peeled prawns, defrosted if frozen, and 125 g (4 oz) spinach. Cook for 3–4 minutes until the prawns are pink and cooked through and the spinach is just wilted.

french onion soup

Serves **4**
Preparation time **15 minutes**
Cooking time **1 hour**

25 g (1 oz) **butter**
2 tablespoons **olive oil**
500 g (1 lb) large **onions**,
  halved and thinly sliced
1 tablespoon **caster sugar**
3 tablespoons **brandy**
150 ml (¼ pint) **red wine**
1 litre (1¾ pints) **beef stock**
  (see page 12)
1 **bay leaf**
salt and **pepper**

Cheesy croûtes
4–8 slices **French bread**
1 **garlic clove**, halved
40 g (1½ oz) **Gruyère**
  cheese, grated

Heat the butter and oil in a saucepan, add the onions and toss in the butter, then fry very gently for 20 minutes, stirring occasionally until very soft and just beginning to turn golden around the edges.

Stir in the sugar and fry the onions for 20 minutes more, stirring more frequently towards the end of cooking until the onions are caramelized to a rich dark brown. Add the brandy and, when bubbling, flame with a long taper and quickly stand well back.

Add the wine, stock, bay leaf, salt and pepper as soon as the flames subside, then bring to the boil. Cover and simmer for 20 minutes. Taste and adjust the seasoning if needed.

Toast the bread on both sides then rub with the cut surface of the garlic. Sprinkle with the cheese and put back under the grill until the cheese is bubbling. Ladle the soup into bowls and top with the cheesy croûtes.

For apple & onion soup, fry the onions as above and add 1 small peeled, cored and grated cooking apple along with the sugar. When the onions are caramelized, flame with 3 tablespoons calvados or brandy then add 150 ml (¼ pint) dry cider, 1 litre (1¾ pints) chicken stock and 2 fresh thyme sprigs. Simmer for 20 minutes. Serve with garlic toasts topped with sliced grilled camembert and sprinkled with a little extra thyme.

russian borshch

Serves **6**
Preparation time **15 minutes**
Cooking time **55 minutes**

25 g (1 oz) **butter**
1 tablespoon **sunflower oil**
1 **onion**, finely chopped
375 g (12 oz) uncooked
  beetroot, trimmed, peeled
  and diced
2 **carrots**, diced
2 **celery sticks**, diced
150 g (5 oz) **red cabbage**,
  cored and chopped
300 g (10 oz) **potatoes**, diced
2 **garlic cloves**, finely
  chopped
1.5 litres (2½ pints) **beef
  stock** (see page 12)
1 tablespoon **tomato purée**
6 tablespoons **red wine
  vinegar**
1 tablespoon **brown sugar**
2 **bay leaves**
salt and **pepper**
200 ml (7 fl oz) **soured cream**
small bunch of **dill**

Heat the butter and oil in a saucepan, add the onion and fry for 5 minutes until softened. Add the beetroot, carrot, celery, red cabbage, potatoes and garlic and fry for 5 minutes, stirring frequently.

Stir in the stock, tomato purée, vinegar and sugar. Add the bay leaves and season well with salt and pepper. Bring to the boil then cover and simmer for 45 minutes until the vegetables are tender. Discard the bay leaves then taste and adjust the seasoning if needed.

Ladle into bowls and top with spoonfuls of soured cream, torn dill fronds and a little black pepper. Serve with rye bread.

For vegetarian borshch with pinched dumplings, soak 40 g (1½ oz) dried mushrooms in 300 ml (½ pint) boiling water for 15 minutes. Make up the soup as above, omitting the beef stock, adding the soaked mushrooms and their liquid plus 1.2 litres (2 pints) vegetable stock (see page 13) instead. For the dumplings, mix 125 g (4 oz) white flour, ¼ teaspoon caraway seeds, salt and pepper, 2 beaten eggs and enough water to mix to a smooth dough. Shape into a sausage, pinch off pieces and add to the soup, simmering for 10 minutes until spongy. Omit the cream and dill.

fragrant tofu & noodle soup

Serves **2**

Preparation time **15 minutes, plus 10 minutes draining**

Cooking time **10 minutes**

125 g (4 oz) firm **tofu**, diced

1 tablespoon **sesame oil**

75 g (3 oz) thin **dried rice noodles**

600 ml (1 pint) **vegetable stock** (see page 13)

2.5 cm (1 inch) piece of **fresh root ginger**, peeled and thickly sliced

1 large **garlic clove**, thickly sliced

3 **dried kaffir lime leaves**, torn in half

2 **lemon grass stalks**, halved, lightly bruised

handful of **spinach** or **pak choi leaves**

50 g (2 oz) **bean sprouts**

1–2 fresh **red chillies**, deseeded and finely sliced

2 tablespoons **coriander leaves**

1 tablespoon **Thai fish sauce**

lime wedges, to serve

Put the tofu on a plate lined with kitchen paper and allow to stand for 10 minutes to drain.

Heat the oil in a wok until hot and fry the tofu for 2–3 minutes until golden brown, stirring frequently.

Meanwhile, soak the noodles in boiling water for 2 minutes, then drain.

Pour the stock into a large saucepan. Add the ginger, garlic, lime leaves and lemon grass and bring to the boil. Reduce the heat, add the tofu, noodles, spinach or pak choi, bean sprouts and chillies and heat through. Add the coriander and fish sauce, then pour into deep bowls. Serve with lime wedges and chilli sauce.

For tofu & satay soup, fry the tofu as above. Add the ginger and garlic to the stock, omitting the lime leaves and lemon grass. Stir in 2 tablespoons crunchy peanut butter and 1 tablespoon soy sauce. Simmer for 3 minutes, then add the tofu, noodles, spinach or pak choi, bean sprouts and chillies. Serve with coriander and lime wedges.

corn & chicken chowder

Serves **4–6**
Preparation time **15 minutes**
Cooking time **about 30 minutes**

25 g (1 oz) **butter** or **margarine**
1 large **onion**, chopped
1 small **red pepper**, cored, deseeded and diced
625 g (1¼ lb) **potatoes**, diced
25 g (1 oz) **plain flour**
750 ml (1¼ pints) **chicken stock** (see page 10)
175 g (6 oz) **canned** or **frozen sweetcorn**
250 g (8 oz) **cooked chicken**, chopped
450 ml (¾ pint) **milk**
3 tablespoons chopped **parsley**
salt and **pepper**
few **red chillies**, sliced, to garnish

Melt the butter or margarine in a large saucepan. Add the onion, red pepper and potatoes and fry over a moderate heat for 5 minutes, stirring from time to time.

Sprinkle in the flour and cook over a gentle heat for 1 minute. Gradually stir in the stock and bring to the boil, stirring. Lower the heat, cover the pan and cook for 10 minutes.

Stir in the sweetcorn, chicken and milk. Season to taste with salt and pepper, cover the pan and simmer gently for a further 10 minutes until the potatoes are just tender. Taste and adjust the seasoning if necessary. Serve the chowder garnished with the sliced chillies and parsley.

For gammon & corn chowder, fry the onion, red pepper and potato in the butter as above. Add the flour then stir in the stock and simmer for 10 minutes. Meanwhile grill a 250 g (8 oz) smoked gammon steak for 10 minutes, turning once then trim off the fat and dice the gammon. Stir into the soup with the sweetcorn, milk and parsley and finish as above.

basque fish soup

Serves **6**

Preparation time **20 minutes**

Cooking time **45 minutes**

2 tablespoons **olive oil**

1 **onion**, finely chopped

½ **green pepper**, cored,
deseeded and diced

½ **red pepper**, cored,
deseeded and diced

1 **courgette**, diced

2 **garlic cloves**, finely
chopped

250 g (8 oz) **potatoes**, cut
into chunks

½ teaspoon **smoked paprika**

150 ml (¼ pint) **red wine**

1 litre (1¾ pints) **fish stock**
(see page 13)

400 g (13 oz) can **chopped
tomatoes**

1 tablespoon **tomato purée**

2 **whole mackerel**, gutted,
rinsed with cold water inside
and out

salt and **cayenne pepper**

Heat the oil in a large saucepan, add the onion and fry gently for 5 minutes until softened. Add the peppers, courgette, garlic and potato and fry for 5 minutes, stirring. Mix in the paprika and cook for 1 minute.

Pour in the red wine, fish stock, tomatoes, tomato purée, salt and cayenne pepper. Bring to the boil, stirring, then add the whole mackerel. Cover and simmer gently for 20 minutes until the fish flakes easily when pressed with a knife.

Lift the fish out with a slotted spoon and put on a plate. Simmer the soup uncovered for a further 15 minutes. Peel the skin off the fish then lift the flesh away from the backbone. Flake into pieces, checking carefully for any bones.

Return the mackerel flakes to the pan. Reheat and ladle into shallow bowls. Serve with lemon wedges and crusty bread.

For Portuguese fish soup, make up the soup as above, omitting the smoked paprika and adding 2 bay leaves. Simmer for 20 minutes without the fish then add 500 g (1 lb) of mixed tuna, cod or hake steaks and 250 g (8 oz) scrubbed closed mussels instead of the mackerel. Cook for 10 minutes or until the mussels have opened then lift out both the mussels and the fish steaks. Flake the fish into pieces, discarding the skin. Remove the mussel shells and discard any closed mussels. Return the fish and mussels to the pan and serve sprinkled with chopped coriander.

index

acknowledgements

Executive Editor Nicky Hill
Editor Kerenza Swift
Executive Art Editor Mark Stevens
Designer Peter Gerrish
Photographer William Shaw
Home Economist Sara Lewis
Props Stylist Liz Hippisley
Production Assistant Vera Janke

Commissioned Photography © Octopus Publishing
Group Ltd/William Shaw apart from the following:
© **Octopus Publishing Group Limited**/Diana Miller 67,
117; Gareth Sambridge 167, 177; Ian Wallace 139; Lis
Parsons 179; Sandra Lane 175, 185; Sean Myers 33;
Simon Smith 25, 29, 47, 87, 105, 181, 207; Stephen
Conroy 16, 79, 101, 121, 163, 193, 199; William Lingwood
39, 51, 191, 213, 231; William Reavell 21, 45, 95, 171,
187, 189, 233.